Discovering British Literature in Bits and Bytes

Discovering British Literature in Bits and Bytes

An Internet Approach

Carolyn M. Johnson

ROWMAN & LITTLEFIELD
Lanham • Boulder • New York • London

Published by Rowman & Littlefield
A wholly owned subsidiary of The Rowman & Littlefield Publishing Group, Inc.
4501 Forbes Boulevard, Suite 200, Lanham, Maryland 20706
www.rowman.com

Unit A, Whitacre Mews, 26-34 Stannary Street, London SE11 4AB

British Library Cataloguing in Publication Information Available

Library of Congress Cataloging-in-Publication Data Available

ISBN 978-1-4758-3825-1 (pbk. : alk. paper)
ISBN 978-1-4758-3826-8 (electronic)

Printed in the United States of America

~To My Mother~

Who always encouraged me in my endeavors
And often offered insightful suggestions

~To My Sister~

For her comments and editorial suggestions

Contents

Preface

What a wonder it is when one types some letters and other characters into a machine and onto a screen, guides a finger or traveling arrow on that screen, and clicks a link or taps search, then suddenly comes upon links that go directly to documents with original texts of words written just so with a personal style and message by authors of long ago, and printed hundreds of years past, or written and published just yesterday or days before then!

It is as wondrous, in its own way, as the wonder that scholars have experienced when discovering a treasure of an actual age-old hand written or printed manuscript or book in an archive or library not readily accessible to a general population. Each is nothing less than a gem discovered in a quarry.

This book and others in the series have been written so that teachers and librarians (both hereafter referred to as educators) can guide the use of the Internet for secondary school students, as well as beginning college or university students, and some middle school students, who are enrolled in basic American literature courses, or perhaps are taking unique courses in English literature. Such courses may include British and American literature from their beginnings through the early twenty-first century.

Volumes in this series include:

- Series 1 (four volumes sub divided into sections) features the beginnings of literature in English, such as early British literature up to and including Chaucer and Spenser, plus British literature just before Shakespeare and after Shakespeare, plus Shakespeare; and the Victorian Era (primarily nineteenth-century British literature), and British literature in the twentieth and early twenty-first centuries)
- Series 2 (four volumes sub divided into sections) features American literature in the beginning, including colonial, seventeenth- and eighteenth-century

American literature; plus nineteenth-century American literature; and American literature (early modern) as well as middle and later twentieth century, the end of the twentieth century, and the beginning of the twenty-first century
• Series 3 (four volumes sub divided into sections) features a miscellany of English literature in special categories, including ethnic American and regional American literature; English literature in the science fiction/fantasy/visionary category and the gothic category; English Literature in nations other than England and the United States, such as Australia, Canada, Ireland, Scotland, Wales, and New Zealand; plus English literature of an uncategorizable and unique but intriguing variety; and English literature considering the future aside from the SF-fantasy-visionary group cited above.

The volumes in this three-part twelve-volume series start at the beginnings of literature in English in places that would become collectively known as England, and in the first flowerings of literature in the United States, in its colonial years; then continue on through the centuries, while including representative works from other English-speaking nations and providing excerpts of representative literary works at the twenty-first century's start; sometimes with ties to earlier works.

The volumes in this series, aim to assist educators in helping students to be introduced to English literature through a medium students like: the Internet. It also aims to introduce educators and students to how English and American literature is represented on the World Wide Web, always with the purpose of encouraging interest, a wanting to discover, enjoy, and learn, as well as be drawn to gaining a sense of critical thinking about English and American literature.

With chapters arranged chronologically, and by literary types, the volumes provide chapters with descriptive titles, introductions based on what is in each featured website on the subject, plus featured websites' urls, as well as questions and activities based on what can be found at the chapters' featured websites, and at additional websites provided in a blog by the author/compiler.

The featured websites are primary-document websites. These primary sites feature full e-texts of, or excerpts from literary works, or a selection of literary works by an author or by genre.

Usually, full e-texts are available for works written before 1930, although there may be exceptions, while works after 1930 will primarily be excerpted texts. Often a first chapter or selected excerpts are featured.

I have created discussion questions and activities to follow the list of featured sites. These questions and activities refer to literary documents found at the featured websites. These questions aim to point to the basic aspects of what each literary document features and to present them in ways that elicit critical thinking.

At the end of each chapter, there is a link to an online list titled "Additional Sites." In each chapter's list, there are: (a) titles and urls with more details on some websites whose urls are listed in chapters' discussion questions and activities; and (b) website titles and urls that link to more websites on the main topic of the primary websites so that additional authoritative sources may be located and research may be accomplished.

Acknowledgments

To some authors writing in english whose lives and works have inspired me, **ESPECIALLY** Emily Dickinson, T. S. Eliot, Madeleine L'Engle, Marianne Moore, Louisa May Alcott, Carolyn Keene, Kathleen McClean, James Redfield, Dan Brown, and more.

CLASSIC AUTHORS—BRITISH

Jane Austen; Anne, Charlotte, and Emily Bronte; Frances Hodgson Burnett; Charles L. Dodgson (aka Lewis Carroll); George Eliot (pen name for Mary Ann Evans Lewes Cross); T. S. Eliot

CLASSIC AUTHORS—AMERICAN

Louisa May Alcott, Rachel Carson, Emily Dickinson, Robert Frost, Marianne Moore, Sarah Orne Jewett

LIBRARIAN—AUTHORS

Beverly Cleary and Madeleine L'Engle, plus: Eleanor Cameron, Eleanor Estes, Mary Downing Hahn, Lilian Morrison, Andre Norton (pen name for Mary Alice Norton), Kit Pearson, Cynthia Rylant, Anne Tyler, Edward Irving Wortis (pen name for Avi).

CLASSIC & WELL-KNOWN AUTHORS FOR CHILDREN / OLDER YOUNG PEOPLE

Kathryn Anderson (aka Kathryn Forbes and Kathleen Mclean), Sheila Burnford, Monica Dickens, Margaret Peterson Haddix, Carolyn Keene (pen name for many writers of Nancy Drew mystery series), Alexander Key, Eric Knight, E. L. Konigsberg, Lois Lenski, Anne Morrow Lindbergh (a daughter of Charles Lindbergh, aka Anne Spencer Lindbergh, Feydy, Sapieyevski, Perrin), Vonda K. Mcintyre, Lucy Maud Montgomery, Scott O'Dell, Phillipa Pearce, J. K. Rowling, Anna Sewell, Elizabeth George Speare, Johanna Spyri, Laura Ingalls Wilder.

PRESENT-DAY AUTHORS NOT NOTED ABOVE

Other authors writing in traditional genre, plus new genres: visionary fiction, time-slip stories.

General Introduction

PART 1: SCOPE OF THE SERIES

English literature, for the purpose of this three-part series of four volumes each, is defined as literature from Britain (especially England, yet also representations from other places in the United Kingdom), from the beginnings of the written language to the present time; as well as the areas now known as the United States featuring generations of European Americans, U.S.-born citizens, as well as some integral ethnic Americans (from first seeds planted in the colonies to the present time). These groups represent features of the authoritative literary canon as well as representative examples of authors or works from the U.S. educational system's Standard Core.

The volumes in the first series include British literature in the beginning with alliterative and accentual verse, metrical runes and riddles, and a letter on the advancement of learning by Britain's King Alfred the Great. The fifteenth, sixteenth, seventeenth, and eighteenth centuries are represented by chapters on Chaucer's *Canterbury Tales* and Spenser's The *Faerie Queene*, John Donne's devotions and epigrams, Samuel Johnson's essays from The *Rambler*, The *Idler* and The *Adventurer*, and Shakespeare's comedies, tragedies, histories, and poetry.

Next, Jane Austen and the late eighteenth and early nineteenth centuries, plus the Victorian era of the middle and later nineteenth century, including works by George Eliot, the Brontë sisters, and Charles Dickens, plus the early twentieth century with T. S. Eliot, Henry James, Alice Meynell, Virginia Woolf, the mid-twentieth century with C. S. Lewis, J. R. R. Tolkien, Dorothy Sayers, Doris Lessing, George Orwell, and more; the later twentieth century and the beginning of the twenty-first century with J. K. Rowling, the new poets laureate, while noting previous British poet laureates in life long positions.

Volumes in series 2 feature American literature—first flowerings (as in poems and essays of Anne Bradstreet and Hector de Crevecoeur) in the seventeenth and eighteenth centuries, nineteenth-century American literature including essays and short stories by Washington Irving; and the first U.S. novelist James Fenimore Cooper, the Fireside poets and Brahmin poets (e.g., Henry Wadsworth Longfellow), and the New England Transcendentalists with the advent of the nature essay by Ralph Waldo Emerson, Henry David Thoreau, and Margaret Fuller; and the second generation represented by Louisa May Alcott, Emily Dickinson, Walt Whitman, and Mark Twain, plus the era of early modern America (from the end of the nineteenth century to the mid-twentieth century and touching the beginning of the century's last quarter), then the mid and later twentieth century and early twenty-first century; all in a variety of literary styles and genres, such as short stories, long fiction, and drama, in addition to poetry and essays; along with specialties including nature essays; critical analysis essays; sonnet poetry; historical fiction; dramatizations of literary works; speculative, fantasy, gothic, and science fiction; and more unique literary works.

Additional volumes in the series provide primary websites plus questions and activities based on representative online examples of ethnic American Literature (such as African American literature (with its main literary movement, the Harlem Renaissance), Asian American literature, Hispanic American literature, Jewish American literature, Native American literature in its various facets, and Scandinavian American literature), plus representations of English literature in nations such as Canada, Australia, New Zealand, Ireland, Scotland, Wales, and South Africa.

American and British literature, including literary gothic fiction (ranging from Mary Wollstonecraft Shelley to Edgar Allan Poe, Louisa May Alcott, Charles Dickens, Henry James, and more), fantasy and science fiction (ranging from Ray Bradbury and Arthur C. Clarke, to Zenna Henderson, Andre Norton, C. L. Moore, Madeleine L'Engle, VernorVinge, plus many more), and visionary literature (with seeds emerging early in places in literature, but primarily in full bloom with the works of, so far, James Hilton, James Redfield, and Michael Gurian), as well as miscellaneous unique subjects, round out the literary representations in this series.

Among the unique subjects in the miscellaneous volume's chapters are Shakespeare and Star Trek, "Dialogue Among Civilizations Through Poetry," U.S. poet laureates, presidential inaugural poets, traditional poetic forms plus "From Politics to Poetics" (a U.S. president turned writer); and classic books brought to life in modern media (as in online video clips) that foster critical thinking on the similarities and differences in each medium. Classic works have played pivotal parts in the early twenty-first century television fantasy, Lost, and, by doing so, draw new generations into the multi faceted marvels of American and British literature.

Also looking uniquely at representatives featured, think of pioneering writers as well as some of their works, with the writers being considered the first literary generations, as matriarchs and patriarchs, while later writers may be thought of as their "literary descendants" (i.e., in particular genres such as poetry, the essay, the novel, and the short story).

"Literary descendants" of previous authors are new authors who have "adopted" something from a classic author and made something of her or his own from it, building on it, or taking up the banner of matriarchs or patriarchs, "grandmothers" or "grandfathers," "fathers" or "mothers," "aunts" or godfathers" of a genre or point of view, and bringing something of the cause into the new millennium—with their own marks on it—with major parts being through the Internet.

Equally marvelous is that many well-known authors' well-known and lesser-known works are readily available. What a surprise and thrill it is to discover that the author of "The Mysterious Key and What It Opened," "A Whisper in the Dark," and "Hospital Sketches," was the writer of great classics for young people; none other than Louisa May Alcott, author of *Little Women* and *Little Men*—AND they can be read online! How intriguing it is to find out that "Gone with the Wind" author Margaret Mitchell also wrote an early novel titled *Lost Laysen*, and a collection of writings recently discovered and published as *Beyond Scarlet: Girlhood Writings of Margaret Mitchell.*

It's also exciting to find out about primary literary descendants (actual relatives of well-known authors), how they are authors in their own right, and how they help to bring their famous ancestors into present times. Note for example, Martha Dickinson Bianchi, the niece of Emily Dickinson, who helped to introduce her aunt's poetic gems to the world; also Reeve Lindbergh who has provided for her mother's book, a foreword to Charles Dickens' great-granddaughter Monica Dickens-Stratton (and her Follyfoot series, plus her Working Chronicles); Thom Steinbeck—son of John—writing his own *Down to a Soundless Sea* and more (e.g., an interesting article "The Boy and His Dog" article at www.thomassteinbeck.com, being more than, yet including, what the title suggests); Madeleine L'Engle's granddaughter Lena Foy writes introductions for reissues of her grandmother's great books, and has published works herself, as is revealed at her website www.lenaroybooks .com; Christopher Tolkien, J. R. R. Tolkien's son, has edited and published his father's writing, as well as publishing his own. J. R. R. Tolkien's daughter

Priscilla has also published articles about her father. J. R. R. Tolkien's grandson Adam Tolkien (son of Christopher) has helped to edit and translate his grandfather's works.

These are just a few of the many literary giants' descendants helping to bring their ancestors' works to new readers, oftentimes making a name for themselves in their own right.

In particular, featured in each volume's chapters, are primary literature documents, how they manifest on the web, and how they may be used to develop critical thinking.

Primary literary documents in cyberspace:

- Actual e-texts, or online reproductions, of novels, short stories, poetry, and essays from the beginnings of oral and written English literature, including classics and little-known works.
- Some rarely seen documents accessible online but not readily accessible to secondary school students in print.
- Some snippets (e.g., quotations, first chapters, excerpts) that are selections from great and lesser known works of modern times—that give an introduction to, a taste of, an enticement for, some work.
- true stories, with their first chapters or other chapters, as online examples.

Features of Websites Useful for Discovering Literature Online and Helping Creative Thinking and Analysis

- Websites with samples of writings such as quotations (including sources noted), excerpts (first chapters, random chapters, selected passages or paragraphs, or first lines or first verses of poetry), such as individual authors' official or authorized websites.
- Websites that provide documents for one author in one place on several pages, such as *Shakespeare on the Internet* and *Shakespeare: A Guide to Shakespeare to the Complete Works*, with e-texts of the plays and poems, plus critical analyses, plus links to documents at other sites; all essential to facilitate critical thinking and analyses.
- Websites with documents by and about several authors in one place on several pages are sources to help critical thinking. Note sites such as the *Luminarium* and its collections of works by, and critical analyses on, medieval, renaissance, seventeenth-century, and eighteenth-century (or Restoration-era) authors. Then there http://www.gutenberg.com and http://www.bartleby.com (an online library of documents that are in the public domain—having been written and published before the 1920s).

- Literary resources websites, including sites of specific literary genres or literary timelines or national literatures (e.g., www.poets.org, *Representative Poetry Online*, and *The Poetry Foundation*).
- Search sites known for providing samples (e.g., http://books.google.com), the ISBN Library (http://digmylibrary.com), www.amazon.com, www.barnesandnoble.com, and more—offer prime material that is "food for thought" or the seeds for critical analyses.
- Other primary documents or authoritative information on the Internet scattered, not yet provided as main websites, are sometimes brought together in the volumes of these series in particular chapters. This is another way for educators to introduce students to literature both well-known and lesser-known, and to the critical analysis process. There may be isolated sites with primary documents that are full texts, or quotations, selected passages, first or random sample chapters, or other types of excerpts. There may also be sites with critical analysis articles or comments.

When all of these are brought together and presented in a chapter, new introductions to works are provided in interesting ways following the purpose of each text in this series. These and other chapters of established main websites provide more opportunities for students' critical thinking through American and British literature, both together referred to as English literature.

SECONDARY AUTHORITATIVE DOCUMENTS WITH REPRESENTATIVES ONLINE

- Research or scholarly papers with critical analysis commentaries; reviews, or introductions, sometimes written by relatives (e.g., Emily Dickinson's niece, Anne Morrow Lindbergh's daughter, Madeleine L'Engle's granddaughter), plus literary executors (e.g., J. R. R. Tolkien's son, Christopher), Thom Steinbeck, son of John, plus scholars, professors, or graduate students of British and American literature, may be taken as authoritative secondary sources.
- Website urls ending in .edu or .org rather than, but not excluding, .com or .net, are usually good indications of websites with accurate facts or authoritative statements backed by quotations and scholars' or other credentialed people's claims or viewpoints.

Note, however, if websites that end in .edu are places where students do assignments online, their accuracy must be double-checked. Also, as with Wikipedia entries (although with good basic data that must also be double-checked), plus essays or term papers written by those just beginning their discoveries (e.g., high school or undergraduate college students doing assignments online for British and American Literature classes). Papers written by writers for term paper companies may be acceptable as starting points also, but what they claim should be verified by other, authoritative sources. Sometimes what is listed in their sources list is a place to start, for example, but students should be guided away from just taking these papers at face value, or else be taught to understand and be capable of evaluating these companies' papers' points of view for themselves.

ONLINE TERTIARY RESOURCES/RESOURCES OF THE THIRD KIND OR LEVEL

Search engines and meta search engines (general and on special subjects), indexes, a webliographies of links that go to primary or secondary documents are the equivalent or modern cyber versions of encyclopedias and indexes.

The Deep Net is also essential to educate students about as they go in search of documents and data on particular subjects.

IN CONCLUSION

This introductory look aims to reveal and point to the aims of this book series—which, primarily, includes ways educators can introduce students to the wonders of literary works written in English, with words imagined years ago and that still have something to say to people living today, as found through the modern medium of the Internet, including well-known works as well as lesser-known works not readily available to students before this modern invention unless they could have access to special archives.

The texts aim to present American literature and British literature (both identified as English literature collectively) as found online in documents or e-texts in ways that spark the interest of young learners to experience the magnificent thoughts and imaginings portrayed in words and in their combinations in sentences and paragraphs and in their intricate designs that are poetry, short stories, novels, and nonfiction essays.

Moreover, this series aims to foster critical thinking, which may be expressed in this way (as suggested at www.edutopia.org/groups/project-learning/8404); besides just remembering information and concepts, people can analyze it, evaluate it, and apply it to the particular works as well as to various life situations.

All this is conducted through this series' chapters' featured websites, these sites' summaries that pinpoint their features, plus questions and activities meant not just for recognizing information, but to spark interest and activate imaginations, as well as develop in intriguing ways: evaluation and critical thinking processes that serve to acquaint students with historical and modern civilizations' magnificent ideas and thoughts, and intellectual as well as inspirational processes, and how it all can be beneficial in their lives.

Narrator/hosts of PBS-TV's *Masterpiece Theater* and *Masterpiece Classic*—which re-creates classic literature for television production—have expressed viewpoints that may be appropriate expressions for the aim of this book, albeit not for the television medium, but that of the Internet.

Laura Linney is known for her portrayal of Abigail Adams (the United States' second first lady) on an HBO series. She has said of her role as a *Masterpiece* host: "Whether it's Austen or Dickens, timeless stories by great authors are worth telling again and again. . . . The beauty of *Masterpiece Classic* is that each generation brings a new and interesting interpretation to these programs."

Alistair Cooke equated his role as host on the *Masterpiece* series with that of a headwaiter. He said, "I'm there to explain for interested customers what's on the menu and how the dishes were composed."

And so it can be where English Literature and the Internet meet, as shown or revealed and guided by entertaining educational works such as *Discovering English Literature in Bits and Bytes*."

Section I

ANGLO-SAXON LITERATURE

Chapter 1

Metrical Charms and Runic Poems

Some of the earliest writings, called charms and runes, were written by ancestors of the people in the land now known as England and were in early forms of the English language.

There are modern English translations from an early form of the English language called Old English, also known as Anglo-Saxon, with yet another later form called Middle English.

Some e-texts of these writings in modern English translations are provided at the *Northern European Studies Texts* website (*Northvegr*).

Some links to e-texts are of modern English translations of twelve metrical charms, including charms for "Unfruitful Land," "A Swarm of Bees," and a "Journey Charm." Charms were meant to ward off bad luck while bringing good luck through a magical power it was believed words had.

Runes, other early writings said to have secret or mysterious messages, include "The Rune Poem" and Cynewulf's runic signature verses in his religious works.

Click the Primary Sources link for Misc. Primary Sources, then the "Rune Poems" link to see modern English titles for poems including the "Anglo Saxon Rune Poem" with broken links not going to translations, but find modern English translations and contemporary examples as cited in urls above for Bruce Dickins, Marijane Osborne, J. R. R. Tolkien, and others.

Under Secondary Sources at the *Northvegr* site, scroll to and click the Runes link, then "Swedish Vikings in England" to read of runes in a modern English document.

On the *Northvegr* home page under Primary Sources, also note its Old English, Texts and Resources, click "Complete Corpus of Anglo Saxon Poetry in Anglo Saxon" link to see title links in modern English to works in the original Old English or Anglo-Saxon language.

Note the additional sites (e.g., a Rutgers University site) with modern English translations.

FEATURED WEBSITES

- http://self.gutenberg.org/articles/Anglo-Saxon_Metrical_Charms   (see descriptions); http://www.northvegr.org
  - Touch Misc. Primary Sources with mouse arrow.
  - Choose "Anglo-Saxon Charms" (see title links in modern English for twelve charms translated from Old English and Anglo-Saxon).
  - Also under Primary Sources, scroll to Misc. Primary Sources, then click link to "Rune Poems" and see titles in modern English for runes written in Anglo-Saxon.
- For e-texts of listed "Rune Poems," scroll to "The Runic Poem" at http://www.arild-hauge.com/eanglor.htm in Anglo-Saxon and in a modern English translation by Bruce Dickins.
  - See a translation for women by Marijane Osborn at www.nordic-life.org/nmh/poem.htm.
  - Under Secondary Sources on *Northvegr*'s main page, click link for "Runes" then "Swedish Vikings in England" to read of runes in a modern English document.
  - For more e-texts of Rune Poems translated into modern English, go to http://www.sunnyway.com/runes/rune_poems.html.
  - Also under Primary Sources at *Northvegr*, touch "Icelandic, Old English, Texts" then click link to "Corpus of Anglo-Saxon Poetry" and title links in modern English to poems in Old English including Cynewulf's "Fates of the Apostles," riddles, charms, and other poems such as "The Riming Poem," "The Seafarer," The Wanderer," and more. Find these and other Anglo-Saxon poems in translation at http://anglosaxonpoetry.camden.rutgers.edu.

- Note Old English literature defined at http://www.cs.mcgill.ca/~rwest/wiki-speedia/wpcd/wp/a/Anglo-Saxon_literature.htm.
- See examples from the recent past at http://alliteration.net/web.htm.

DISCUSSION QUESTIONS AND ACTIVITIES

1. Find and read e-texts of modern English translations of three examples of early English writings called charms.
   a. Find these e-texts online at the "Anglo Saxon Metrical Charms" page at a featured website as stated above.

b. Choose a charm meant to help someone going on a "Journey," a charm meant to help an "Unfruitful Land," a charm meant to help someone caught up in a bee swarm.

c. Quoting from each charm, identify what the narrator in each charm aimed to say, and how he or she expressed it.

2. Choose two charms in e-texts of modern English whose translations you find online.

a. Choose one charm found in a featured website as cited in summary and url above.

b. Choose another charm at any site cited in the related Internet sites area below.

c. Write an essay.

d. Identify what the narrator aimed to say, and how he or she expressed it.

e. Quote from each charm to support what you claim.

3. Find and read two modern English e-text translations of the Old English "Rune Poem."

a. Follow links as directed in the featured sites summary above to find e-text of a traditional rune, translated with men in mind, as with Bruce Dickins's translation.

b. Find another rune's e-text translation online with women in mind; as with one translated by Marijane Osborn at a featured site cited above.

c. From each translation above, choose and identify three words: one about nature, one about a thing, and one on a person or people.

d. Quote some phrases (in translation) that the poet used to express something of what each word represents.

e. Identify one passage each from the poems, then compare both translations of it, as you consider each narrator as s/he presented the subject for women or men.

4. Find and read some definitions of runes on the Internet.

a. Look for definitions found online as cited under "Runes Defined" in the related sites area below. Note what is on the "Runic Alphabet" web page and pages found via its links and the "Viking Runes Through Time" web page.

b. Choose some definitions of runes.

c. Quote from the chosen definitions as you briefly identify what runes are.

5. Keep in mind the "Rune Poem" and definitions of runes referred to in questions/activities nos. 3 and 4 above.

a. Suggest how runes may have other meanings (maybe hidden "under the surface").

b. Quote phrases from some of the rune poems to support what you claim.

c. Keep in mind as an example the "Rune Poem" and its traits as sample traits of runes.

6. Find and read an e-text of a Modern English translation of Cynewulf's runic signature verses and his "Fates of the Apostles."
   a. Find a modern English translation online (e.g., at the Poetry Foundation website as cited in Additional Websites below), and note some critical analyses.
   b. Note the whole work but pay attention to lines 20 through 23.
   c. Identify words that are main runic symbols or alphabet letters.
   d. Tell which runic words identify Cynewulf and how.
   e. Identify the runes' subjects.
7. Study again online definitions of rune, and the runic alphabet, found as cited in question/activity 4 above.
   a. Being guided by the way Cynewulf wrote his runic signature verse, select some runic letters.
   b. Write a poem that you can call your own "runic signature" verse.
   c. Tip: Use one letter (the first in your name), or some or all letters of your name.
8. Find an e-text document titled On "Mimicking Old English Verse Forms in Modern English," plus "The Very Nature of Alliterative Verse," "J. R. R. Tolkien's Alliterative Poems," and Modern Alliterative Poetry.
   a. Find and read the first e-text and the last cited e-texts at, or through links at, the *Forgotten Ground Regained* website. Find other sites as cited in the related sites area below.
   b. Write a brief essay in which you identify how someone may create an approximation of Old English verse according to this document.
   c. Consider, for example, a key that captures what, while keeping what else?
   d. Identify four suggestions on what to look out for, or aim to do and not do.
   e. Read e-texts excerpts from J. R. R. Tolkien's works, then write an essay suggesting how Tolkien used the key and the four suggestions in these e-text excerpts of his works.
   f. Read other alliterative poetry from the recent past. Tell how they show alliterative traits.
9. Literary charms are still around in a way in modern times, as shown in Harry Potter stories.
   a. Write an essay in which you suggest how some charms in the Harry Potter stories are similar in their purpose to actual charms in early English.
   b. To gather information for your essay, find some what may be called realistic charms and spells and their types defined, then where and how they are presented in the Harry Potter books, as cited at websites on Harry Potter in the additional sites below.

c. Define charms and spells according to the Harry Potter worldview, and tell why they are done and how to do them. Use quotes from the books when possible.

d. Describe, for example, from the Harry Potter books, the counter-charm for hiccups, a spell to reenergize a person, or another spell or charm.

e. Choose a charm or spell in book one or two, then in another book.

f. Tell what the chosen charm is, why it is done, who does it, and what the outcome is.

Additional websites for chapter 1, with more data to note

- https://clynjohnson.wordpress.com
  - Click link to "Discovering English Literature . . . Additional Websites," then link to a wordpress.com blog at netedbooks, or go directly to http://www.netedbooks.wordpress.com/blog.

Chapter 2

Old English and Early
Middle English Verse

To find online translations of Old English and early Middle English language writings of British literature into early Modern English (e.g., by Ezra Pound, and others), visit the first featured website *Forgotten Ground Regained* and click links.

Each translation offers a sample of ancient Britain's literary world and actual world. Sometimes more than one translation of the same work challenges students to see similarities or differences among various translators' interpretations.

Find links on the Other Translations page to selected writings in the original early English and in modern English translations, such as *Beowulf* (1000 AD) by an unknown anonymous author or Scribes A and B in a monastery, the Pearl Poet's *Sir Gawain and the Green Knight* (1400 AD) (with references to King Arthur), and more.

Click the Medieval Poetry link in left column to go to a page of links to, William Langland's *The Vision of Piers Plowman* (1337–39? AD) in early English.

Note the Site References link on the left that brings up links on the right to other areas (e.g., Electronic Texts Archives) and their links to other websites (e.g., *Luminarium*, with its modern English translation of *Piers Plowman*).

Click also on the Poetic Techniques link in the left column to go to links on the right under From the Editor, to, Linking Letters: *A Poet's Guide to Alliterative Verse* (especially parts 3 and 4) for an introduction to the poetic technique dominant in early English (i.e., Old English and Early Middle English) writings.

More links on the right of Poetic Techniques page under Elsewhere On Web go to more data in Overviews, Old English Alliterative Verse, other subjects (e.g., J. R. R. Tolkien & Alliteration).

Note also in *Poetic Techniques* and *Essays* areas, links to Richard Moore's "Poetic Meter in English: Roots and Possibilities," Paul Deane's "Alliterative Poetry and J. R. R. Tolkien," and Dana Goia's essays "Accentual or Alliterative Verse" and "Poetry As Enchantment."

FEATURED WEBSITES

- http://alliteration.net
  - Click Other Translations link under Resources in left column and click links under the headings titled Old English and Middle English. For interesting definitions of poetry in general, click Poetic Techniques and *Essays.*
- http://alliteration.net/Pearl.htm
  - See excerpts from *Sir Gawain and the Green Knight.*
  - Note link to Corpus of Middle English Works at http://alliteration.net/original.htm with some modern English translations at http://alliteration.net/translate.htm.
- Excerpts from *Beowulf* at http://alliteration.net/beoIndex.htm and https://web.archive.org/web/20150816194203/http://beowulftranslations.net/index.html.
- Note data on J. R. R. Tolkien and alliteration at http://alliteration.net/ALLITERT.HTM, http://alliteration.net/Beleriand.htm, and at http://alliteration.net/technica.htm see Dana Goia's "Accentual Verse," and "Poetry As Enchantment."
- The Great Vowel Shift at http://facweb.furman.edu/~mmenzer/gvs/lit.htm

DISCUSSION QUESTIONS AND ACTIVITIES

1. Find and read online explanations of alliteration, the poetic form in which early English poetry was primarily written, in the early versions of the language called Old English (also called Anglo-Saxon) and Middle English.
   a. Find online explanations at the http://alliteration.net featured website after clicking Poetic Techniques under Resources, then clicking the Anglo-Saxon Alliterative Verse link and Alliteration link. See explanations at http://alliteration.net/fieldgd.htm in *Linking Letters: A Poet's Guide to Alliterative Verse* (especially parts 2 and 4), found also through A Field Guide to Alliterative Verse link at the http://alliteration.net via the *Editor's Notes* page and see a definition attributed to J. R. R. Tolkien on the Tolkien and Alliterative Verse page found through the http://alliteration.net Editor's Notes page.

b. Write a definition of alliterative verse from the data you find online.

c. Choose a poetic e-text example of alliteration from a modern English translation of early English verse (i.e., from Old English or Early Middle English verse). You may choose to explain a translated excerpt from the *Historical Prologue* of *Sir Gawain and the Green Knight*, part 2 (especially lines four through sixteen), or a translated excerpt from *Beowulf*, both found through links under Classic Works at http://alliteration.net and *Beowulf* translated by Francis Gummere at https://ebooks.adelaide.edu.au/b/beowulf/b48g and more at http://www.beowulftranslations.net/alliteration.html.

d. Tell how alliteration is expressed in the poetic passage you chose.

e. Also find more data at websites through the link cited below for *Additional Websites*.

2. Find and read online definitions and examples of a kenning (a literary device used in Old English or Anglo Saxon literature).

a. Formerly found through the *Poetry Magic* link at http://alliteration.net/outside.htm, see http://www.poeticbyway.com/gl-k.html and its definition of kenning.

b. Visit also the websites *Kennings and BEOWULF*, *Kennings and Anglo Saxon Literature*, and *Eddic and Skadic Kennings*, cited in Additional Websites below.

c. List three definitions of a kenning.

d. Provide two examples each of modern translators' translations of kennings, such as those by Seamus Heaney, Bertha Rogers, and others.

3. Find and read excerpts that are online Modern English translations of parts of William Langland's *Piers Plowman*, such as the B-Text Excerpts.

a. Find excerpts online at the *Luminarium* website through the http://alliteration.net featured website's Site References link, found as cited above.

b. Note the translation of the Prologue, especially lines 1 through 19.

c. What did the narrator decide to do, and when, but what happened instead?

d. Identify some of the "fair field of folk" the narrator sees, including especially but not exclusively the folk in the lines following line 19.

e. Suggest how alliterative verse helps the poet's message (even in translation) to be told.

f. Scroll to bottom of the page (near page 6) and tell of a warning narrator gave.

4. Find and read e-text excerpts in a modern English translation of *Beowulf*.

a. Find these e-texts online as cited in http://alliteration.net/beoIndex.htm and https://web.archive.org/web/20150816194203/http://beowulftrans

lations.net/index.html featured websites cited above, then by clicking chapter links.

   b. Click the link for *The Haunted Mere*, then scroll to the third verse and read excerpt.

   c. Write a paragraph including quotations from the alliterative lines.

   d. Identify features of the place and two trekkers.

   e. What does the narrator ask someone to do? What will he give him if he does it but only if something happens (which you should identify).

5. Find and read e-text excerpts from a modern English translation of the Pearl Poet's *Sir Gawain and the Green Knight*.

   a. Find these e-texts online at http://alliteration.net/Pearl.htm featured website page.

   b. Click link in the left column for *The Green Knight Arrives.* Read verses 7 through 13.

   c. Quoting alliterative phrases that you can find in this translation, tell what is going on when the Green Knight comes in. Describe three of his many features.

   d. How do people in the room react? What is the reaction of an important person? Who is it? What is the challenge (but not a fight) that the Green Knight suggests to this person?

6. Keep in mind question/activity 5 above and the story referred to in it.

   a. Click the link at http://alliteration.net/index.htm for Gawain Takes Up the Challenge.

   b. Scroll to and read verses 14 through 21.

   c. Quoting alliterative phrases, tell how Gawain described his connection to the important person the Green Knight spoke to.

   d. Tell what Gawain asks to do and why.

   e. How did the important person respond?

7. Find and read online definitions of epic poetry.

   a. Find these definitions at Aristotle—Poetics—Epic Poetry and Definition of Epic Poetry pages at www.sacred-texts.com/cla/ari/poe/index.htm (xxiii, xxiv, and xxvi).

   b. Write a definition of epic poetry. Draw from what you find at sites cited above.

   c. Write an essay in which you suggest how *Beowulf, Piers Plowman*, or *Sir Gawain and the Green Knight* may be thought of as an epic.

8. Find and read online definitions of Dream Vision Poetry.

   a. Find these definitions online at http://faculty.goucher.edu/eng240/dream_vision.htm and other websites found via link for Additional Websites cited below.

b. Write a brief description of dream vision poetry.

c. Read excerpts from online translations of Old English and early Middle English works identified as dream vision poetry, such as parts of *Piers the Plowman* and *The Pearl*, *Dream of the Rood*, and Geoffrey Chaucer's *House of Fame* and *Parliament of Fowles*.

d. Tips: Find works at or through the featured alliteration.net site via the Medieval Poetry link in the left column, or via the Site References link, then Electronic Texts Archives and Reference Sites link, then Luminarium link and its links to Medieval Resource including bartleby.com's Prosody of Old and Middle English Verse, and its Alliterative Revival, plus links going to amazon.com's dream vision poetry work titled *The High Medieval Dream Vision: Poetry, Philosophy and Literary Form* (1988) by Kathryn L. Lynch with a definition and explanation in the introduction.

e. Suggest how these poems show features of dream vision poetry as identified in the descriptions at the websites referred to just above.

9. Find and read websites with data about the Old English era and Middle English era.

a. Find these sites, such as for the *Norton Anthology of English Literature*, pages at the http://www.ucalgary.ca/uofc/eduweb/engl401/faq.htm, www.anglo-saxons.net/hwaet, http://www.thehistoryofenglish.com/timeline.html (note 1385 and 1450 etc.), http://historialenguainglesa .blogspot.com/2012/12/timeline-of-middle-english-period-1100.html, plus http://facweb.furman.edu/~mmenzer/gvs/lit.htm, http://vos.ucsb. edu/browse.asp?id=2740, and other sites on these eras, their society, literature and authors, in some Additional Web Sites for chapter 2 via the link at https://wordpress.com/posts/carolynlibrarianwriterword presscom.wordpress.com.

b. Write an essay in which you tell something of the time period from 500–1500 AD or CE—the times when Old English and Middle English literature were being created.

c. Cite literary and related cultural features.

d. Suggest how, you think, the Old English era and the early Middle English era are different, similar, separate, or overlapping.

e. Write an essay giving an overview of features, reasons, and seven events (in 1066, 1362, 1385, 1399, 1450, 1476, and 1500), that marked a period of time; before, during, and just after the great vowel shift. What did it signal the end of, and the beginning of? Which literary works were important then? How? Why?

Additional websites for chapter 2 with more data to note

- https://clynjohnson.wordpress.com
  - Click link to "Discovering English Literature. . . . Additional Websites," then link to a wordpress.com blog at netedbooks), or go directly to http://www.netedbooks.wordpress.home.

Chapter 3

Colloquy

On a page featuring Anglo-Saxon links at the website for *The Heroic Age: A Journal of Early Medieval Northwestern Europe*, see links to pages of some of the earliest literary works in the English language, written as the English language emerged, at the time when the first ancestors of people in today's England lived.

These works were written in early versions of the English language known as Anglo-Saxon, also called Old English, or were translated from Latin into Old English.

Old English texts or modern English translations are provided through links at this site.

These early writings, both poetry and prose, expressed people's basic concerns of those times, such as hard living and death, war, and religious subjects.

Note links in the *Anglo Saxon Literature* area to *Anglo-Saxon Literature* (1884) by John Earle and *Anglo-Saxon Narrative Poetry Project*. See also works' links under authors' names, plus links under particular Anglo-Saxon works such as the *Vercelli Book*.

FEATURED WEBSITES

- http://www.heroicage.org/as.php
  - Scroll to links under Literature and its sections.
  - Note working links in English to documents in Anglo-Saxon, Old English, or modern English translations.
  - Note links under Aelfric, such as *Of Seasons of the Year*; link to Bede.net and its link to isasweb.net and its link to web searches.
- See Ann Watkins's translation of a colloquy at www.kentarchaeology.ac/authors/016.pdf.

DISCUSSION QUESTIONS AND ACTIVITIES

1. Find and read an e-text of a modern English translation of a colloquy by Aelfric, written during the late tenth century or early eleventh century.
   a. Find modern English translation online at Ann Watkins' www.kent archaeology.ac/authors/016.pdf (a featured website cited above):
   b. What did a student say to a teacher?
   c. What did the teacher ask? What did the student answer?
   d. Write your own colloquy between yourself or someone else of your age and a teacher, parent, or other adult.
2. Find and read e-texts of modern English translations of *Caedmon's Hymn*, written about 670.
   a. Find these e-texts online by clicking links at the Heroic Age featured website http://www.heroicage.org/as.php.
   b. Scroll to find link to *Caedmon's Hymn*, an Old English Version by Heorot. Click Heorot link to view introduction, then click link to text and modern English translation.
   c. Back on the main featured website http://www.heroicage.org/as.phpcited above, click link to Bede's Account of Caedmon and CAEDMON'S HYMN as translated into modern English in 1990 with Old English examples by Kevin Kiernan.
   d. Identify what, according to Bede, happened to Caedmon in a dream.
   e. Compare phrases in two or more modern English translations of the *Hymn* at the http://www.heroicage.org/as.php website, such as one translated from an early version of English called *Northumbrian* and one from Bede's Latin version.
   f. Compare, the different words used for the first and second parts of each line.
   g. Next, identify, how God is identified, how works, wonders, roof, middle earth, and people, or words similar to them, are referred to.
3. Find and read an e-text of a modern English translation of Bede's poem whose first line starts with the phrase "Before the inevitable journey," also known as "Death Song," written in 735.
   a. Find translation via http://www.heroicage.org/as.php featured website that goes to Bede.net and its web search links, then search for first line at Google Books.
   b. Identify who the poem's narrator believes will be the wisest human being if that person thinks about what and when.
   c. Provide suggestions you think of that you see as examples of what Bede wrote about.

4. Find and read an e-text of a modern English translation of Aelfric's *On the Seasons of the Year*, written during the late tenth century or early eleventh century.

   a. Find a translation online by clicking the title link under Aelfric under Literature at the *Heroic Age* featured website http://www.heroicage .org/as.phpcited above.

   b. List the subjects he wrote about.

   c. From various paragraphs on different seasonal subjects, identify different types of winds he mentioned, the metaphor he used to describe the Earth, and his views of stars.

   d. Choose another subject he wrote about, and then tell, while quoting, something important or interesting from paragraphs he commented in about this subject.

5. Keep in mind Aelfric's *On Seasons of the Year* referred to in question 4 above.

   a. Look at this textbook's chapter 1 on Selected Anglo Saxon [Old English] Literature such as metrical charms and Runes, plus something by Gildas.

   b. Identify how Aelfric's writings, although on subjects similar to subjects in the Anglo-Saxon metrical charms, are written in a different way.

6. It is stated at http://www.medievalchurch.org.uk/p_aelfric.php (via chapter 3, *Additional Sites* at https://netedbooks.wordpress.com/home, click link to chapter 3 list), that "As Alfred was the founder, so Aelfric was the model, of the Saxon prose."

   a. Suggest why you think this statement may be true.

   b. Quote from Aelfric's writings that you find online to support your viewpoint.

   c. Tip: Scroll to find links to more of Aelfric's works at http://www.hero icage.org/as.php.

   d. Find, modern English translations of Aelfric's preface to his *Grammar* and his preface to *First Series of Catholic Homilies*.

   e. Identify what John Earle wrote about Aelfric in 1884 in his Anglo-Saxon Literature, found online via the link at the Heroic Age featured website above under Literature.

   f. Quote from e-texts of excerpts from Aelfric's works, and from comments about Aelfric by Earle, to support and provide examples for your answer to b) above.

Additional websites for chapter 3 with more data to note

- https://clynjohnson.wordpress.com
  - Click link to "Discovering English Literature. . . . Additional Websites," then link to a wordpress.com blog at netedbooks), or go directly to http://www.netedbooks.wordpress.com/home.

Chapter 4

A Letter on the Advancement
of Learning

At the Bucknell University featured site, after scrolling to and clicking the translation title link, see the web page that features an e-text of a modern English translation by an unnamed author of King Alfred's Letter on the Advancement of Learning as sent to a Bishop of Werfrith.

It was sent then in the form in which it appears here as the 894 Prose Preface to Pope Gregory's book (first published in Latin in the year 591). The book was considered to be a guide by Gregory, who was both a spiritual leader and teacher.

It was translated into early English by King Alfred, who is identified by scholars as "the father of english prose." Alfred translated the work into the form of early English known as Anglo-Saxon English or Old English.

The document features the thoughts of Alfred, also known as Aelfred, identified as the first English monarch, although he reigned in just a part, but an important part, of what is now present-day England, a place called Wessex, in the southwest part of the nation.

The document shows, in essay and letter form, the concern (the first by an English monarch) about learning and knowledge for his nation's people in the beginning years of the nation now known as England, the main nation of Great Britain.

Serving as examples of this monarch's literary aims and cultural goals for his people, e-text samples of King Alfred's prose and poetry can be found at the Bucknell University website, plus the websites with *King Alfred's Poems Now Turned into English Metres,* his *Preface to St. Augustine's Soliloquies,* and *King Alfred the Great and His England.*

FEATURED WEBSITES

- www.departments.bucknell.edu/english/courses/engl440/pastoral.shtml
  - ○ Click link to *Modern Translation to Alfred's Prose Preface of Pastoral Care* (note also links to Alfred's Old English prose version of this document).
  - ○ See *Preface to St. Augustine's Soliloquies* fccs.ok.ubc.ca/__shared/assets/Modern_English_Translation3522.doc.
  - ○ Click search icon for close-up view at https://archive.org/details/kingalfredspoem00tuppgoog of *King Alfred's Poems* and flip pages with mouse arrow or click at bottom right of each book page.
- An epitaph in his own words at http://www.england-history.org/2012/09/king-alfred-the-great-and-his-england.
- Scroll to paragraph 14 to the phrases "The earliest work Alfred commanded to be translated . . ."; "He, himself, assisted by his scholars, translated . . ."

DISCUSSION QUESTIONS AND ACTIVITIES

1. Find and read an e-text of a modern English translation of King Alfred's *Prose Preface* to his early English translation of *Pope Gregory's Pastoral Care*.
   a. Find this e-text online at the featured Bucknell University web page, www.departments.bucknell.edu/english/courses/engl440/pastoral.shtml cited above.
   b. Study the first paragraph.
   c. Identify which kinds of men Alfred said once lived in England before his time.
   d. What were the *sacred orders* some men were eager about?
   e. Why did men come from abroad (other nations) to England at that early time?
   f. What was so interesting about men from abroad at the time Alfred wrote his document? Why?
   g. What was Alfred thankful for as he wrote?
   h. What did he ask be done by the bishop he wrote to?
2. Study e-text of paragraph 2 of a modern English translation of *Alfred's Prose Preface* to his early English translation of *Pope Gregory's Pastoral Care*.
   a. Find this e-text online at the featured Bucknell University web page, www.departments.bucknell.edu/english/courses/engl440/pastoral.shtmlcited above.

    b. Tell what Alfred also remembered, especially with reference to England's churches and yet why this was of little benefit.

    c. How did Alfred use footprints as a metaphor?

    d. What did Alfred say had been lost and why?

3. Study paragraph 3 of a modern English e-text translation of Alfred's Prose Preface to his early English translation of *Pope Gregory's Pastoral Care*.

    a. Find this e-text online as the featured Bucknell University web page, www.departments.bucknell.edu/english/courses/engl440/pastoral .shtml cited above.

    b. What did Alfred wonder about with reference to some men in England and what they would not do, and why they would not do it (in part because they could not conceive of something that happened, which you should identify).

4. Study paragraph 4 of a modern English e-text translation of Alfred's Prose Preface to his early English translation of *Pope Gregory's Pastoral Care*.

    a. Find this e-text online at the featured Bucknell University web page, www.departments.bucknell.edu/english/courses/engl440/pastoral .shtml cited above.

    b. What did Alfred say some other people of other nations did?

    c. Identify what it seemed better to him that he and other Englishmen should do? Why?

    d. What did he see "if there was peace," that would be good for England's youth to do, until they could accomplish what?

5. Study paragraph 5 of a modern English e-text translation of Alfred's Prose Preface to his early English translation of *Pope Gregory's Pastoral Care*.

    a. Find this e-text online at the featured Bucknell University web page, www.departments.bucknell.edu/english/courses/engl440/pastoral .shtml cited above.

    b. Why did Alfred start to translate something into English (actually the early form of English known in his time)?

    c. What did Alfred translate?

    d. Which two goals did he sometimes aim for; really one or the other; as he translated?

    e. What else did Alfred do "when I had," "just as I had," and "as I could do most?"

6. Find and read an e-text of the *Bishop of Sherbourne's Biography of King Alfred*, written in 888, in a modern English translation.

    a. Find an e-text of this translation online at http://omacl.org/KingAlfred and click links to Introduction, Parts One and Two. See description via Additional Websites cited below.

    b. Study the first paragraphs suggested.

    c. Identify a challenge young Alfred's mother gave to him and his brothers when Alfred was growing up.

    d. What was the prize his mother planned to offer to the winner of the challenge?

    e. How did young Alfred react to what his mother suggested?

    f. What was a wish Alfred had starting at an early age?

7. Find and read an e-text of what an early twentieth-century scholar, John Richard Green, wrote of Alfred.

    a. At http://www.ensignmessage.com/kingalfredthegreat.html, after scrolling 3/4 down the page, find e-text of these statements. See pages 99–105 at https://archive.org/details/historyenglishpeo01gree. More data at Sites cited below.

    b. What did Professor Green write on Alfred's interests for himself and his people? These interests were other than his interests in religious and political matters.

    c. In which literary genre was he most interested?

    d. What did Alfred aim to do?

    e. Find and read e-text excerpt of a translation of Alfred's translation on Boethius' *Consolations of Philosophy*, found at http://www.royal.gov.uk/pdf/alfred.pdf and described in Additional Websites as cited below.

    f. Comment more on Alfred's aims with quotes in Alfred's translation of Boethius' work.

8. Find and read the e-text of the first page of an article on Alfred's talking poetry and other e-texts of works about and with examples of Alfred's poetry.

    a. Find this e-text at *King Alfred's Talking Poems* by James W. Earl (1989) at http://www.jstor.org/stable/1316601?seq=1#page_scan_tab_contents.

    b. Do you agree, or not, with Earl's statement of Sisam's evaluation of Alfred's verse? Why? or why not?

    c. Quote from translations of Alfred's poetry to support your answer.

    d. Read some of Alfred's poetry as translated by and commented on by Martin F. Tupper in *King Alfred's Poems* (1850) at https://archive.org/details/kingalfredspoem00tuppgoog (click search icon, flip pages with arrow). See notes in additional websites cited at https://netedbooks.wordpress.com/home.

    e. Quote from one or more of these poems, and Tupper's comments, as you suggest the importance of Alfred's poetry and particular poems.

    f. Find, study, Winston Churchill's 1956 comment on Alfred in a document's e-text at http://charltonteaching.blogspot.co.uk/2010/10/greatest-englishman-ever-king-alfred.html.

    g. Quote Churchill and suggest how his comment supports positive view of Alfred's poetry.

9. Find and read e-text excerpts of a modern English translation to *King Alfred's Old English Translation of St Augustine's Soliloquies* (with *A Rendering into Modern English*).
   a. Find this e-text at fccs.ok.ubc.ca/__shared/assets/Modern_English_Translation3522.doc.
   b. Scroll to and read parts (2v), (3r), and (3v).
   c. What are the two books called "soliloquiorum" about?
   d. What account did the narrator give of them?
   e. What or who did the narrator think answered him?
   f. What did "she" say to him?
   g. In a dialogue, what did he and "she" talk about?
   h. Which two points noted in the conversation make the word "entrust" important?

10. Find and read more excerpts from an e-text of a modern English translation of the last words of St. Augustine's *Soliloquies* that was translated into Old English by Alfred; noting especially at the end of the work the first phrase of the line that starts "Therefore me thinks. . . . ."; then find and read the e-text of a quote from Alfred's last writing titled *Blotsman*.
    a. Find an e-text translation in modern English of Alfred's Old English translation of the *Soliliquies* and Alfred's *Preface* at www.gutenberg.org/files/40341/40341-h/40341-.htm.
    b. See also a quote from Alfred's last writing *Blotsman* (an anthology) at the websites http://www.england-history.org/2012/09/king-alfred-the-great-and-his-england and http://www.leslettreseuropeennes.eu/wp-content/uploads/2013/04/GHILLEBAERT_English-literature_part-I.pdf.
    c. Suggest what the sentence from *Blotsman*, aka *Blooms*, means?
    d. Why do scholars identify this sentence, referred to in c) above, as a fitting tribute to King Alfred?
    e. What do you think the last sentence of Alfred's translation of Book III of St. Augustine's *Soliloquies* may mean?
    f. Why may the document referred to in e) above also be thought of as a tribute?

Additional websites for chapter 4 with more data to note

- https://clynjohnson.wordpress.com
  - Click link to "Discovering English Literature… Additional Websites," then link to a wordpress.com blog at netedbooks, or go directly to http://www.netedbooks.wordpress.com/home.

Chapter 5

Riddles from "The Exeter Book" (970–1042) by Anonymous

Some early English writings, called riddles, were written in early versions of the English language. This early version of the English language is called Old English (aka Anglo Saxon, with West Saxon and Northumbrian dialects), plus Early Middle English verse.

See examples of these riddles, called Exeter Riddles, the beginnings of English literature, at featured websites with translations in modern English plus some original Old English texts.

Note translations of nearly one hundred riddles that were collected with other writings in a manuscript called "The Exeter Book," and preserved by a Bishop Leofric, who donated it to the Exeter Cathedral in 1042.

See translated riddles, try to identify what each refers to, then look at the answers.

The riddles may be numbered differently with, for example, number 42 (at first featured site) is identified as number 45 (at second featured site), and number 47 (at third featured site).

Featured websites cited below feature Exeter riddles translated by scholars. Note translations by Megan Cavall and Matthias Ammon; Paul F. Baum (c) 1963, with explanations offered by Alfred John Wyatt (1835–1935); five riddles with commentaries to introduce students to analyzing riddles; and Joseph Barone with links to hidden riddle answers, now broken.

A sign of the enduring nature of the literary format of the riddle is that riddles are present in English literature even today, as studies of, and examples from, Tolkien's The *Hobbit* and Rowling's Harry Potter books reveal, as in *Riddles in The Hobbit* and *Riddles of Harry Potter*.

Scholars through time have translated, studied, and written commentaries on the riddles.

See some of their writings online at www.oenewsletter.org/OEN/index
.php, at various university sites such as the California State University and
the University of Toronto websites and at additional sites, for which a link is
cited at the end of this chapter.

FEATURED WEBSITES

- https://theriddleages.wordpress.com/riddles-by-number
  - See links to fifty Exeter riddles by numbers going to OE versions, mod-
    ern English translations, answers and commentaries.http://www.swarth
    more.edu/Humanities/english/oldenglish
  - See number links for the selected riddles 45, 76, 25, 23, 27, click transla-
    tion links, then commentary links.
- http://www.technozen.com/exeter
  - Click links to number groups of riddles, then individual numbers (ques-
    tion mark cluster links to answers are broken).
  - Click a subject link at https://en.wikisource.org/wiki/Anglo-Saxon_Rid
    dles_of_the_Exeter_Book, then links for number groups, then individual
    numbers, then a riddle, its answer, and an explanation.
- http://www.csun.edu/~sk36711/WWW/355/nelson.pdf
  - See functions of the Exeter riddles), http://homes.chass.utoronto.
    ca/~cpercy/courses/1001Brewer.htm; http://www.thing.net/~grist/ld/
    young/ky-bkrid.htm, http://www.csun.edu/~sk36711/WWW/355/nelson
    .pdf.

DISCUSSION QUESTIONS AND ACTIVITIES

1. Find and read translated e-text excerpts of, and data online about, the
   Exeter Book riddles.
   a. Find data at the http://www.swarthmore.edu/Humanities/english/old
      english featured site.
   b. In other featured websites and in the additional websites online and
      cited below at https://netedbooks.wordpress.com/home (click chapter
      five link).
   c. At http://www.thing.net/~grist/ ld/young/ky-bkrid.htm, see defini-
      tions by Karl Young; see Hazel Brewer's comments at University of
      Toronto's http://homes.chass.utoronto.ca/~cpercy/courses/1001Brewer
      .htm; Gerard Benson at http://wonderingminstrels.blogspot
      .com/2001/12/bookworm-anonymous.html; University of Glasgow's
      http://theses.gla.ac.uk/2943/1/2011diganmphil.pdf with Laura Digan's

introduction; Marie Nelson at the University of Florida's http://www.csun.edu/~sk36711/WWW/355/nelson.pdf; Michael Alexander's *Old English Riddles from the Exeter Book* at http://books.google.com; plus Kevin Crossley-Holland's *Nature of the Riddle* at amazon.com, Craig Williamson's *Introductions to, and Translations of, the Riddles in "BEOWULF and Other Old English Poems"* at amazon.com; S. A. J. Bradley's *Introduction* to *Anglo-Saxon Poetry* at amazon.com; and others cited in the additional websites below.

    d. Write a short essay in which you identify main features of riddles.

    e. Note, for example, Ms. Nelson's four functions of the riddles and two types of riddles' challenging endings; plus Mr. Young's quote "Most riddles open with. . . ."

2. Find and read an e-text of a Modern English translation of "riddle 47" from the Old English book titled "The Exeter Book."

    a. Find this e-text at the https://theriddleages.wordpress.com/riddles-by-number and http://www.technozen.com/exeter featured websites.

    b. Study the riddle.

    c. Write a paragraph in which you aim to identify what the riddle means.

    d. Note: Be sure to quote some of the riddle's phrases to provide examples of the riddle's meaning and to show how you understand it.

    e. For help with the riddle's meaning, look for its key word at another featured site, or find an alternate translation and answer at another site cited in additional websites on the Internet as cited below at https://netedbooks.wordpress.com/home (click chapter 5).

    f. If you guess a solution/answer to the riddle, or if you find a suggested answer or solution and choose to accept it, write your paragraph explaining why you support the interpretation.

3. Find and read an e-text of a modern English translation of "riddle 26" from the Old English, *The Exeter Book*, found at https://theriddle ages.wordpress.com/riddles-by-number and http://www.technozen.com/exeter.

    a. Study lines 13 through 28 (including a part that starts with a phrase about being clothed and a part that starts with the words "If the children of men will use me").

    b. Study the riddle, then write a paragraph suggesting what you think the riddle means.

    c. Include some of the riddle's phrases to provide examples of the riddle's meaning and to show that you understand it.

    d. For help with the riddle's meaning, see other e-texts of a modern English translation of this riddle (also identified as XXVI) at another featured site or in additional websites at https://netedbooks.wordpress.com/home as cited below.

    e. If you guess an answer or solution to the riddle, or find a suggested answer or solution, and choose to accept it, write your paragraph explaining why you support this interpretation.

4. Find, read, e-text of a modern English translation of "riddle forty nine" from the Old English, "The Exeter Book," found at the https://theriddle ages.wordpress.com/riddles-by-number and http://www.technozen.com/exeter featured websites.

    a. Study the riddle and think about its meaning.

    b. Write a paragraph identifying what you think the riddle means.

    c. Quote some of the riddle's phrases to provide examples of the meaning and to show your understanding of it.

    d. For help with the riddle's meaning, see the *Riddle Ages* featured website at https://theriddleages.wordpress.com/riddles-by-number/, and other e-texts of modern English translations of this riddle as found at another featured website or in "additional websites" at https://neted books.wordpress.com/home as cited below.

    e. If you guess an answer or solution to the riddle, or you find a suggested answer or solution and choose to accept it, write a paragraph explaining why you support the interpretation.

5. Find and read e-texts of modern English translations of the *Exeter Book* riddles 91 and 44, found at the http://www.technozen.com/exeter or https://theriddleages.wordpress.com/riddles-by-number featured websites.

    a. Quote from the riddles and identify the narrators' features.

    b. Write a paragraph identifying what you think the riddles mean.

    c. Quote some of the riddles' phrases to give examples of the meaning, especially in ways that show you are aiming to understand it.

    d. For help with meaning, see other e-texts of these riddles' modern English translations as found at the other featured sites or at additional websites at https://netedbooks.wordpress.com/home as cited below.

    e. If you guess an answer or solution to the riddles, or if you find a suggested answer or solution and choose to accept it, write your paragraph explaining and showing, while including quotations, why you support this interpretation.

6. Keep in mind what you discovered when doing questions/activities 1, 2, 3, 4, and 5 above.

    a. Write a short essay.

    b. In this essay, suggest how these riddles are connected.

7. Keep in mind what you did in questions 2, 3, 4, 5, and 6 above.

    a. Choose another riddle from "The Exeter Book" that you find by number at the https://theriddleages.wordpress.com/riddles-by-number and http://www.technozen.com/exeter featured websites, by

subject then number at the https://en.wikisource.org/wiki/Anglo-Saxon
_Riddles_of_the_Exeter_Book featured website, by subject/title at
the additional website, http://elfinspell.com/RiddlesandGnomicVerse.
html, or in various ways at other additional websites such as http://
www.dmoz.org/Arts/Literature/World_Literature/British/Old_English/
Individual_Poems/Exeter_Book_Riddles.

b. Identify what the chosen riddle means or to what it refers.

c. Be sure to quote some of the riddle's phrases as examples pointing to
what you think this riddle means.

d. If you guess an answer or solution to riddle, or find a suggested answer
or solution, and choose to accept it, write your paragraph explaining
why you support this interpretation.

e. Alternately, choose from among these riddles: 8, 24, 33 (especially
lines 1–8), 34, 39 (especially lines 1–4, 21–27, 56, 69, and 85, or
another number); or from the Baum book: Natural Phenomena 7, Birds
22, Miscellaneous 57, Domestic Subjects, Other Animals, Writing,
Music 44, Chiefly Christian 12, and others.

8. Riddles or the synonym-like runes can also be found in the modern writings of J. R. R. Tolkien, such as *The Hobbit.*

a. Find three riddles from this work, found online at http://hubpages.com/
literature/The-Riddles-In-The-Hobbit-Riddles-In-The-Dark-Answers;
www.tolkientrail.com/riddles.shtml;   http://www.carlanayland.org/
essays/riddles_word_games.htm; and more in additional websites at
https://netedbooks.wordpress.com/home as cited below.

b. You may use at least one or all of the riddles that start "a box without
hinges," "this thing all things devours," "it cannot be seen," or choose
other ones.

c. As you did with the ancient riddles, study these riddles, then write paragraphs in which you aim to identify what the riddles mean.

d. Be sure to quote some of the riddle's phrases to provide examples of
the riddle's meaning, especially ones that show how you understand it.

e. Tip: If you guess an answer or solution to the riddle, or find a suggested answer or solution, and choose to accept it, write your paragraph
explaining why you support this interpretation.

9. Riddles or their synonym-like runes can be found not only in writings
from English literature's beginnings, you can also find them in the Harry
Potter books popular today.

a. Find and read the first page of chapter 1, and pages 9 and 10 of Shira
Wolosky's *The Riddles of Harry Potter: Secret Passages and Interpretive
Quests* found online after a title search at www.amazon.com and click-
ing the "look inside this book" link and/or doing a search for riddles.

    b. Identify the importance of riddles in general and in connection with Harry Potter.

    c. Read the riddle by the third door found online at the '*JK Rowling Lexicon*' website, http://www.hp-lexicon.org/about/sources/jkr.com/jkr-com-door-instructions.html.

    d. As you did with the ancient riddles, study this riddle, then write a paragraph in which you aim to identify what the riddle means.

    e. Be sure to quote some of the riddle's phrases to provide examples of the riddle's meaning, especially ones and in ways that show how you understand it.

    f. If you guess an answer or solution to the riddle, or if you find the suggested answer or solution and choose to accept it, write a paragraph explaining why you support this interpretation.

    g. Be sure (as guided by additional websites below) that riddles found online are really Rowling's riddles from the Harry Potter books, such as the sample referred to just above.

    h. Who was the character Percival Pratt and what did he have to do with riddles?

10. U.S. President Theodore Roosevelt had a favorite riddle.

    a. Find an e-text of this riddle at http://www.innovateus.net/innopedia/history-riddles or http://en.wikipedia.org/wiki/Riddle#Charades.

    b. Choose a phrase from this riddle.

    c. Suggest why it is a good example of what the riddle refers to.

11. Think about or look again at what you discovered when doing question 1 above.

    a. Be guided by what you read or thought was written about riddles in general.

    b. Be guided by numbered riddles cited in other questions in this textbook's chapter.

    c. Think of, then write, a riddle of your own in poem or paragraph form.

Additional websites for chapter 5 with more data to note

- https://clynjohnson.wordpress.com
  - Click link to "Discovering English Literature. . . . Additional Websites," then link to a wordpress.com blog at netedbooks, or go directly to http://www.netedbooks.wordpress.com/home.

Chapter 6

Selections from "The Exeter Book"

At the website called *Forgotten Ground Regained: Translations of Alliterative and Accentual Poetry*, see introductions to the beginnings of English literature featuring poetry.

See links to various translations into modern English of early English writings that were written in early versions of the English language, such as Old English (also called Anglo-Saxon, with West Saxon and Northumbrian dialects) and Early Middle English verse.

Click left column's Other Translations link. Find links in right column to translations into modern English of Old English poems collected in one of English literature's first books, called "The Exeter Book," featuring more than 150 items including poems, riddles, and religious writings and so titled because it was given to Exeter Cathedral Library in 1042 by preserver Bishop of Leofric.

At the *Forgotten Ground Regained* website, see links to long poems including "The Wanderer," "The Seafarer (975 AD)," "The Ruined City," "The Wife's Lament," "The Husband's Message," "Rhyming Poem," and more, with translations in modern English by J. R. R. Tolkien, Ezra Pound, Eric F. J. Martin, Sean Miller, and others.

Click Site References link for links to more translations. See literal or commonsense translations by Bella Millett, Chauncey B. Tinker, Ann Stafford, Michael R. Burke, Ellen Amatangelo, and Charmae Cottom.

See other translations cited in other featured sites above, and additional websites below.

See new examples in OE style in modern English by recent poets. See W. H. Auden, C. S. Lewis, G. M. Hopkins, Seamus Heaney, and others at *Modern Revival*, alliteration.net site, plus an OE version of *Alice in Wonderland* written by a nineteenth-century scholar.

FEATURED WEBSITES

- http://alliteration.net/translate.htm
  - Click title links for selected *Exeter Book* poems.
- http://www.northvegr.org/index.html
- At https://unr440.wordpress.com/2015/09/03/the-exeter-book-introduction-and-contents
- https://web.archive.org/web/20040607073404/http://www.georgetown.edu:80/labyrinth/library/oe/exeter.html
  - see modern English title links to OE versions of *Exeter Book* entries; for the *Rhyming Poem* in a 1922 translation go to https://archive.org/details/jstor-27702657, click other formats link then html or PDF link;
- for more selected *Exeter Book* poems, see
  - http://www.southampton.ac.uk/~enm/widsith.htm;
  - http://www.elfinspell.com/EarlyEnglishHusband.html;
  - http://research.uvu.edu/mcdonald/Anglo-Saxon/wife'slament/wifeothertrans.html
  - http://anglosaxonpoetry.blogspot.com/2012/04/order-of-world.html
  - https://unr440.wordpress.com/2015/09/15/the-exeter-book-the-order-of-the-world
  - See also *Modern Poetry* link at http://alliteration.net
  - https://en.wikipedia.org/wiki/Alliterative_verse#Modern_revival

DISCUSSION QUESTIONS AND ACTIVITIES

1. Find and read Eric F. J. Martin's modern English translation, in an e-text format, of the Old English poem titled "The Ruined City."
   a. Find this e-text online by clicking the title link in the featured website at http://alliteration.net/translate.htm.
   b. Study the last eleven lines of part 3, then lines 1 through 6.
   c. Identify who is referred to, what mood they were in, how they were dressed, and which seven things they gazed at, then identify what else the narrator imagined that once was in this place. Study the first part, line 4 and identify what is referred to.
2. Keep in mind the e-text of a modern English translation of *The Ruined City*, found as cited in question/activity 1 above.
   a. Study part 2, lines 1 through 13.
   b. Identify what still endures and shines, yet what has changed and how.
   c. Study part 1, lines 2, 11, and 15, plus part 2, lines 4, 9, and 19, then part 3, lines 7, 10, 16, and 17.

    d. Tell what the narrator identified as reasons why the city became a "waste place" of ruins (including three types of reasons and examples of each).

3. Find and read an e-text translation in modern English of excerpts from an early English-language work titled *Concerning the Ruin of Britain* (written about 540) by Gildas.

    a. Find it online directly at http://www.northvegr.org/index.html and by following links at http://alliteration.net for site references, Anglo-Saxon and Norse Literature, Personal Home Pages, Sean Miller's Anglo-Saxon site and its What's Elsewhere links area and its link to Voice of the Shuttle. Then scroll to and click VOS link to *NetSerf*, then click link to NetSerf Resources, then search at *NetSerf* for Old English or Anglo-Saxon, then do Google web search for *Works of Gildas*, click *Northvegr* link, then Histories and Chronicles link, then works of Gildas for his works in translation.

    b. Study the excerpts from chapter 23.

    c. Identify to which particular happenings or people the writer compared, in a metaphoric way: wolves in a sheep fold, a lioness's lair, darkness and the mind, talons, brood, offspring, germ, room, plants, dogs, leaves, and branches.

    d. Study the excerpts from chapter 25.

    e. Identify to which happenings and people the writer compared bees and their hives.

    f. Study the first part, then the second part of excerpts from chapter 26.

    g. Identify who and what the writer suggested as patterns for people.

    h. Tip: Provide quoted phrases to illustrate what the writer was referring to.

4. Find and read an e-text of a modern English translation (e.g., Sean Miller's) of the Old English poem "The Wanderer."

    a. Find this e-text by clicking title link at http://alliteration.net/translate .htm.

    b. Find and read online definitions and examples of a kenning (a literary device used in Old English or Anglo Saxon literature), at http://www.poeticbyway.com/gl-k.html, http://www.cyberartsweb.org/cpace/ht/knots/Kennings.html, http://www.davidgsimpson.com/ref/kennings .pdf, http://literarydevices.net/kenning, https://vikingsbooksetc.word press.com/2013/03/21/skaldic-poetry-and-eddic-poetry (scroll to "Skaldic poetry also involves especially prominent use of kennings"); then list three definitions of a kenning and provide two examples each of modern translators' translations of kennings, such as those by Seamus Heaney, Ezra Pound, and Robert Frost.

    c. Study "The Wanderer," especially lines between about 8a and 16a.

    d. Identify what the narrator refers to in the line that begins "I know it truly," while referring to two examples of a kenning.

    e. Study lines around 46a through 72a.

    f. What happens when the narrator refers to the mind surveying something?

    g. What do the spirits of seafarers never bring back?

    h. What does the narrator think about his spirit when he ponders on the life of people throughout the world?

5. Study further the e-text of the modern English translation beside the OE version of "The Wanderer," found online by clicking title link at http://alliteration.net/translate.htm.

    a. Study especially lines 46a through 72a, found as cited in question 3 above.

    b. Keep in mind that J. R. R. Tolkien quoted part of this poem in his *Lord of the Rings* stories, as stated at the bottom of the featured website cited just above.

    c. What is so about Middle Earth? Why can't a man call himself wise? What must a wise man be, not be, and before what?

    d. Study lines 88a through 96a.

    e. What does the narrator say of "he who thought wisely" and "pondered deeply"?

    f. Study lines 100a through 112a.

    g. What does the narrator say about "the famous fate" and how nature is involved?

6. Keep an e-text of a modern English translation of "The Wanderer" in mind, online by clicking the title link at the featured website, http://alliteration.net/translate.htm.

    a. Choose a passage from this translation.

    b. Find another modern English translation or two not used in questions 3 and 4 above and found online as cited in the *additional websites* section below.

    c. Quote some phrases from the chosen passage as you tell how the passage's meaning may be different and similar because of translators' individual interpretations.

7. Find and read an e-text of a modern English translation of the Old English poem "The Seafarer" (e.g., Sean Miller's), found by clicking title link at http://alliteration.net/translate.htm.

    a. Study the beginning of the poem through about line 16a, then study lines around 16a through about 24a, and around line 52a.

    b. What does the narrator say about himself? Identify some examples he gave.

    c. Tell which seven birds he mentioned and what he liked about them, instead of what else.

    d. Study lines around 28a through about 40a and 44a through about 52a.

    e. How does the narrator compare sea life and life on the land?

    f. What does a land dweller "credit little" about a seafarer's life?

    g. What does the seafarer say about the life he lived?

    h. Study around lines 72a through 80a.

    i. What did the narrator see as "the best epitaph"?

    j. Study lines just past line 108a, plus lines around line 116a and some following lines.

    k. Identify four things that man must keep and be, then what is greater and who is mightier than any man's thoughts, and what should be pondered.

8. Still keep in mind an e-text of a modern English translation of "The Seafarer", found by clicking the title link at http://alliteration.net/translate.htm.

    a. Choose a passage from it.

    b. Find another modern English translation or two not used in question/activity 6 above. Search sites cited in the additional websites below.

    c. Quote some phrases as you tell how the chosen passage's meaning may be different and yet similar because of the translators' individual interpretations.

    d. Compare a phrase translated by Miller with one translated by Ezra Pound, found by following a link, then searching via http://alliteration.net/translate.htm, or go directly to http://rpo.library.utoronto.ca/poems/seafarer.

9. Find and read an e-text of a modern English translation of the poem "Widsith."

    a. Find this e-text, for this other work in *The Exeter Book*, as provided in 2003 by Bella Millett at http://www.southampton.ac.uk/~enm/widsith.htm.

    b. Study lines 1 through 7, 50 through 56, 94 through 108, 130 through 134, then 135 through 139.

    c. As you quote phrases from this poem, identify what the main character did when he spoke, where he went, what he did on his travels and when he came back, then what he said about his occupation.

10. Find and read an e-text of a modern English translation of "The Wife's Lament."

    a. http://research.uvu.edu/mcdonald/Anglo-Saxon/wife'slament/wifeothertrans.html find a modern English e-text translation by Robert E. Diamond.

    b. Study verse 1 (except the last line).

    c. Why is the wife as narrator writing this poem?

    d. Study verses 2 and 3.

    e. Why is the wife's husband absent? What does the wife try to do? What obstacles must she cope with? Why?

    f. Study the last line of verse 1, and line 20 and the last three lines of verse 3, and the last two lines of the last verse (verse 5).

    g. Quote from the poem as you tell about what bothers the wife.

    h. Study lines 1 through 7 of the poem's last verse.

    i. Quoting some phrases, identify two situations, one of which the wife thinks may be the reason for her husband's continued absence. How does she believe he is reacting to it?

11. Keep question/activity 10 above in mind as you find and read an e-text of a modern English translation of "The Husband's Message."

    a. Find this e-text online at http://www.elfinspell.com/EarlyEnglishHusband.html.

    b. Suggest how, as scholars have commented, this poem answers "The Wife's Lament."

    c. Suggest why the message, or the object on which it is delivered, as narration or narrator, is effective.

12. Find and read an e-text of a modern English translation of "The Rhyming Poem."

    a. Find this e-text at the https://archive.org/details/jstor-27702657 featured web page.

    b. Study lines 1–35, 40–42; 36–39, 43–69, and 70 with the following lines, especially 73–74.

    c. Write an essay. What is the narrator saying in each group of lines? Suggest how one part of a line works with another line part to define and show examples of what he wants to say.

13. Find and read excerpts from e-text of a modern English translation of "Order of the World."

    a. Find the translation at http://anglosaxonpoetry.blogspot.com/2012/04/order-of-world.html.

    b. It is claimed that this poem, in part, "provides the reader with a complex depiction . . . a self-portrait . . . of the Anglo-Saxon poet . . . influenced by themes of . . . self-assurance, exploration and the power of poetry as a craft," plus something of the religious.

    c. Read the third stanza and scan other lines in this thirteen-stanza poem.

    d. Write an essay. Quote from the third stanza and from other parts of the poem's translation, as well as from the quotation in b) just above.

Describe how a portrait of an Anglo-Saxon poet is depicted, what "the power of poetry" is, and how that power affects that poet.

e. Tell how this poem helps you understand the first English poets and their writings.

14. Read modern creations of poems written in the style of Old English poetry.

a. Click the *Modern Poetry* or *Fantasy Poetry* link at http://alliteration .net/index.htm featured site. Look for poems by J. R. R. Tolkien, G. M. Hopkins, Ezra Pound, P. K. Page, and others.

b. Choose one poem by one of these modern poets.

c. Write an essay. Suggest the features from Old English poetry that you find in this modern poem. Suggest why the modern poem written in the format of Old English poetry helps to convey what the poet wanted to say.

Additional websites for chapter 6 with more data to note

- https://clynjohnson.wordpress.com
  - Click link to "Discovering English Literature . . . Additional Websites," then link to a wordpress.com blog at netedbooks, or go directly to http:// www.netedbooks.wordpress.com/home.

Section II

FOURTEENTH, FIFTEENTH, AND SIXTEENTH CENTURIES—POETRY

Chapter 7

Selections from
The Canterbury Tales

It is thought that the fourteenth-century English writer Geoffrey Chaucer, who lived from 1343 until 1400, was the first author to write literary works in the English language, especially his *The Canterbury Tales*. By doing this, he transformed this language from a language only for illiterate or lower-class people into a literary language equal to that time's other literary languages such as Latin and Italian.

Manuscript of the parts *Tales* were distributed and read in the 1380s but first published in 1476.

E-texts of two original versions plus authoritative user-friendly versions now exist and are provided online. Original Caxton versions are at a featured British Library web page. A Harvard University featured website has e-texts of the *Tales* in an original Middle English version with lines in modern English interwoven in an "interlinear version," with each line's translation placed below the line it translates. Sections' side-by-side original and modern English versions are at libirius.com.

A reader-friendly version has modernized spelling, explains unusual words at right of the text and in a glossary, and is in an e-document by Michael Murphy of Brooklyn College, part of the City University of New York. *The Prologue* in the original English plus links to explanations of unusual words can be found at the *Librarius* featured website and the Brooklyn College site with modern explanatory English words in the right margin.

More featured sites to assist studies of Chaucer and his works in e-text format include The Electronic *Canterbury Tales* companion, *Essays and Articles on Chaucer* at the *Luminarium* website; at *the Chaucer MetaPage*; plus a *Chaucer Glossary* to medieval English words and modern English equivalents.

FEATURED WEBSITES

- www.bl.uk/treasures/caxton/homepage.html
  - Two original Caxton versions in old type with explanation of Caxton's English, www.libarius.com/cantales.htm.
  - See original Caxton version with original words but in modern type and see side-by-side section translations of Middle English and modern English at www.courses.fas.harvard.edu/~chaucer/teachslf/tr-index.htm.
  - See interlinear translations with one line then a translation, then another line and a translation; see e-text of modernized spelling version with unusual words explained at right of text at http://academic.brooklyn.cuny.edu/webcore/murphy/canterbury/2genpro.pdf.
  - See modern English at left and Early English at right, section by section, of the Tales at http://pages.towson.edu/duncan/chaucer/duallang1.htm.
- "General prologue" to the *Tales* with links to explanations of unusual words at www.librarius.com/cantales/genpro.htm and through link at *Chaucer Online/Electronic Canterbury Tales Companion* at http://www.kankedort.net;
- Chaucer as "Father of English Poetry," commentaries on tales, at www.courses.fas.harvard.edu/~chaucer/special/authors/dryden/dry-intr.html and at www.bartleby.com/190/8.html (scroll to last third of fifth paragraph at page's bottom);
- www.luminarium.org/medlit/chaucessays.htm see links to essays/articles on Chaucer;
- *Chaucer Glossary* at www.literature-dictionary.org/Chaucers-Middle-English-Glossary;
- *MetaPage* with links to more sites http://englishcomplit.unc.edu/chaucer/index.html.

DISCUSSION QUESTIONS AND ACTIVITIES

1. Find and read an e-text in a modern English translation of the "General Prologue" to *The Canterbury Tales* by Geoffrey Chaucer.
   a. Find a literal translation at the featured Harvard University website cited above or look for a poetic translation at another featured website. Note versions at the Brooklyn College, Towson College, and *Librarius* featured websites.
   b. Identify, including quotations, what, according to the narrator, inspired people to go on pilgrimages, and when, as he stated in the first section of the prologue.

2. Keep in mind Chaucer's prologue to his *Canterbury Tales*, as referred to in the Harvard University, Brooklyn College, Towson College, and *Librarius* featured websites.
   a. Identify what the narrator said in the first part of the last part of the prologue about the way he will tell the tales of the people who are going on a pilgrimage.
   b. Do you agree or disagree, in whole or in part, with what he said? Comment on why you think this way.
   c. Identify what the narrator says was said by the ancient philosopher and writer Plato. Comment on why Plato's comment is important.

3. Keep in mind Chaucer's prologue to his *Canterbury Tales* and the narrator's descriptions of the people going on a pilgrimage, as referred to in the featured websites at Harvard University, Brooklyn College, Towson College, and *Librarius*.
   a. Identify the people who will go on the trip.
   b. Choose three of the travelers, then quote a few phrases that the narrator used to describe each traveler you chose.
   c. Why do you think these quoted words give very vivid descriptions of each traveler?
   d. Tip: Identify a knight, a squire, a prioress, a wife of Bath, or a clerk, and some others, and then choose any of them as the three travelers of your choice.

4. Still keep in mind Chaucer's prologue as referred to in the Harvard University, Brooklyn College, Towson College, and *Librarius* featured websites.
   a. How did the narrator/host choose the first traveler to tell a tale?
   b. How did the chosen traveler react to his being the first in the group to tell a story?
   c. Imagine you, or some person of note, being chosen as the first tale teller during a trip.
   d. How would you react, or how do you think the person you chose would react?
   e. Would the tale you tell, or the tale the person you chose would tell, be influenced by being the first tale teller? Why or why not?

5. Scholars say Chaucer's *The Canterbury Tales* may be called a representation of the people and society of his time.
   a. Keep in mind basic features and characters of Chaucer's *The Canterbury Tales*.
   b. Imagine a trip today taken by a group of people. Suggest where today's travelers may go, why, and how.
   c. Identify three to six people in this group. How may they represent today's society?

    d. Suggest a story each person in the group could tell the others during the trip.

    e. Tips: For one person, write a poem that introduces or starts a story that she or he might tell; for another person, write, in poem or story form, a tale that he or she might tell.

6. Think of the women described in the prologue to *The Canterbury Tales* as referred to in question/activity 3 above.

    a. Compare the women travelers. Tell what you think of them (i.e., how they may be representative of the women, or some women, in the society of Chaucer's time).

    b. Is there a type of woman of that time who may not be represented among the travelers?

    c. Compare some of the women travelers with some of the women in the tales (e.g., Cecilia, Ypolita and Emily, Prudence, Griselda, Dorigan, Guinevere and an old woman, and Custance, in the tales told by the Second Nun, the Knight, Melibee, the Clerk, Franklin, Wife of Bath, and Man of Law).

    d. Suggest a type of woman you think may not be represented in the tales.

7. Find and read an e-text in a modern English translation of "The Canon's Yeoman's Tale," one of *The Canterbury Tales* by Geoffrey Chaucer.

    a. Find an e-text online at the Brooklyn College featured website, http://academic.brooklyn.cuny.edu/webcore/murphy/canterbury/2genpro.pdf.

    b. Note especially in the first part the references to the search for the philosopher's stone in lines 309 through 325, with special attention to the last eleven lines in this passage.

    c. What does the thing cause seekers of the stone to do? What comes, however? Where? How?

    d. What is hard? What should one be warned about? What is usually the result or outcome?

8. Keep in mind Chaucer's "Canon's Yeoman's" Tale, found as cited in question 7 above.

    a. Note, in the tale's second part, references to the philosopher's stone's secret recipe (i.e., in lines 889 through 918).

    b. Identify what people should not busy themselves with, unless philosophers do what?

    c. Why did he say it or quote someone who said it?

    d. Identify what should be kept secret. Why?

    e. What, did the storyteller say, are philosophers sworn to do?

    f. Who is the one who should know and why?

    g. Why do you think, what the storyteller said or quoted, makes sense or has good points?

9. Find and read an e-text, in a modern English translation, of Chaucer's prologue to "The Nun's Priest's Tale," and then "The Nun's Priest Tale" (another of the *Canterbury Tales*), found online at the Brooklyn College featured website http://academic.brooklyn.cuny.edu/webcore/murphy/canterbury/2genpro.pdf.

   a. Including quotations, identify what, in response to the previous tale teller's story, the knight said is a bad tale and a good tale, then identify the host's phrase that refers negatively to the previous tale teller's tale.

   b. Next, tell about the story that the nun's priest told.

   c. Tips: Identify the tale's main character, what predicament he found himself in, and how he was able to get out of that bad situation. What comments did he make that are called morals (i.e., something important that one can learn from the tale)?

10. Find and read an e-text, in a modern English translation of "The Manciple's Tale," another *Canterbury Tales* by Geoffrey Chaucer.

    a. Find this e-text online at the Brooklyn College featured website http://academic.brooklyn.cuny.edu/webcore/murphy/canterbury/2genpro.pdf.

    b. Who is a manciple?

    c. What did he say about a caged bird?

11. Find and read, in a modern English translation, an e-text of "The Parson's Tale," another one of Geoffrey Chaucer's *Canterbury Tales*.

    a. Find this e-text online at the Brooklyn College featured website, http://academic.brooklyn.cuny.edu/webcore/murphy/canterbury/2genpro.pdf.

    b. Of what did this traveler want to remind the other travelers?

    c. Suggest what you believe he meant and then what his statement means to you.

    d. Support your comments with examples you think of from your life, the lives of people you know, or other people in today's society.

12. Literary critics, including John Donne of the seventeenth century and Sir Arthur Quiller-Couch of the twentieth century, claimed Chaucer was the father of English poetry.

    a. Find claim at www.courses.fas.harvard.edu/~chaucer/special/authors/dryden/dry-intr.html featured web page with comments by John Dryden and comments in the fifth paragraph from the bottom of the page at the www.bartleby.com/190/8.html featured web page of *On Lineage of English Language* by Quiller-Couch.

    b. Identify comments Donne and Quiller-Couch stated to support their view.

    c. Quote from *The Canterbury Tales* to illustrate and support what both critics claimed.

Additional websites for chapter 7 with more data to note

- https://clynjohnson.wordpress.com
  - Click link to "Discovering English Literature . . . Additional Websites," then link to a wordpress.com blog at netedbooks, or go directly to http://www.netedbooks.wordpress.com/home.

Chapter 8

Selections from *The Faerie Queene*

At the *Edmund Spenser Online* website offered by England's Cambridge University, click links under Scholarly Resources to online texts, a critical bibliography, a biography, and a discussion list, for this noted sixteenth-century renaissance-era English writer living 1522–1599.

See also links to critical analysis periodicals including *Spenser Review* with links to issues online, plus *Spenser Studies* with abstracts/synopses of its issues' articles; and more.

On the online text pages, note a link to a website such as *Renascence Editions* (now at http://www.luminarium.org/renascence-editions/fqintro .html and at *Scholars Bank* at the University of Oregon website, https:// scholarsbank.uoregon.edu/xmlui/handle/1794/784). Also note the Spenser Page at the University of Toronto Library's *Representative Poetry Online* now at http://rpo.library.utoronto.ca/poets/spenser-edmund.

Note also the University of Vermont's *Spenserians* website's translation with original English and detailed descriptions of the various parts of *The Faerie Queene*.

At http://search.lib.virginia.edu/catalog see the University of Virginia's Modern English Collection with link to *Spenser's Works*, such as his poems, sonnets, and *The Faerie Queene*, all featuring e-texts in an early English language.

See also e-texts for *The Shepheardes Calendar, Complaints Containing Sundrie Small Poems of the Worlds Vanitie,* including *Cantos of Mutabilitie, Fowre Hymnes,* and more.

See critics' views at *Luminarium*'s *Renaissance Essays: Edumund Spenser* and other sites, and note C. S. Lewis's commentaries cited and quoted in featured web sites just below.

FEATURED WEBSITES

- www.english.cam.ac.uk/spenseronline/welcome
  - See links for *Spenser Review, Spenser Studies*, and *Scholarly Resources Online Texts*, or go directly to *Renaissance Edition*'s *Faerie Queene* at http://www.luminarium.org/renascence-editions/fqintro.html.
  - Or *Scholar Bank*'s *Faerie Queene* at https://scholarsbank.uoregon.edu/xmlui/handle/1794/784.
- See Spenser's stories retold for young readers by Jeanie Lang (n.d.) at www.gutenberg.org/files/41350/41350-h/41350-h.htm and by Mary McCleod (1916) at www.sacred-texts.com/neu/eng/sfq.
- See e-texts of the prologue for Spenser's *Faerie Queene* at http://www.sca.org.au/bardic/vocal/poems/a_gentile_knight.html and http://www.sacred-texts.com/neu/eng/fq/fq03.html.
- See versions of *Faerie Queene* meant to make the meanings and language of the tales more accessible at http://spenserians.cath.vt.edu/TextRecord.php?textsid=35115.
  - Click author, click titles, and note http://spenserians.cath.vt.edu/TextRecord.php?textsid=34525, with notes from *The Faerie Queene: A New Edition with a Glossary, and Notes Explanatory and Critical* 1758 by John Upton, and note revisions cited at www.amazon.com; http://anthony.sogang.ac.kr/books/Ren3.htm (see some modern English words in margin). See reading guides for *Faerie Queene* at https://www.gutenberg.org/files/6930/6930.txt, http://socrates.acadiau.ca/courses/engl/rcunningham/2273/FQ-ReadingAid.html, and https://en.wikisource.org/wiki/The_Faerie_Queene/Book_I/Glossary.
- See critics' views at http://www.luminarium.org/renlit/spenseressay.htm via links and at http://web.archive.org/web/20030220153900/, http://www.dbu.edu/mitchell/spensers.htm.
- See C. S. Lewis on Spenser in *Studies in Medieval and Renaissance Literature* (1966) after book title search, search inside book for Spenser, at www.amazon.com (e.g., page 146) and in phrases (e.g., Lewis's statement on critical interpretations "only use" quoted in highlighted box, then Lewis's tracing "Spenser's understanding of natural growth" at center of medievalmvb's dissertation) at https://medievalmvb.wordpress.com/2014/06/18/reading-c-s-lewis-on-spensers-use-of-allegory-in-the-faery-queene. Spenser and Literary Devices at https://prezi.com/9jhbrcyfzak2/literary-devices-of-the-faerie-queene, https://orangemanor.wordpress.com/2010/08/12/spenser%E2%80%94the-faerie-queene, and www.theartsjournal.org/index.php/site/article/download/126/123.

- Spenserian sonnet defined at http://www.literarydevices.com/sonnet, http://www.sonnets.org/basicforms.htm and http://www.sonnets.org/glossary.htm#195.
- Spenserian Stanza defined at www.english.emory.edu/classes/Handbook/Spenserian.html, http://andromeda.rutgers.edu/~jlynch/Terms/spenserian.html, and http://www.gutenberg.org/files/15272/15272-h/15272-h.htm#Intro_III.4.
- Title links to Spenser's poems at www.sanjeev.net/poetry/spenser-edmund/index.html and at *Representative Poets Online,* http://rpo.library.utoronto.ca/poets/spenser-edmund and http://www.poetryfoundation.org/bio/edmund-spenser (click poems link, then title links).

DISCUSSION QUESTIONS AND ACTIVITIES

1. Find and read an e-text of book I of Edmund Spenser's *The Faerie Queene.*
   a. Find this e-text online at http://www.luminarium.org/renascence-editions/fqintro.html or https://scholarsbank.uoregon.edu/xmlui/handle/1794/784, both accessible formerly through links for online pages at the *Spenser Online* featured website cited above.
   b. Identify seven main characters, their names and characteristics, what they represent or personify, and what is each one's purpose.
   c. Provide quotations to support your claims.
   d. Hint: Read of the traits of one main character as told by other main characters, in book I, canto ix, verses 13 through 16, and in book II, canto ix, verses 3 through 6, as told by another main character.
2. Keep in mind Spenser's portrayal of the character of the Faerie Queene, as referred to in question/activity 1 above:
   a. Identify a noteworthy person of the present or recent past.
   b. Write a poem suggesting how this person may influence or have an effect on someone, maybe you or someone like you, and cause that someone to do something, either directly involving that person or something that person represents.
3. Find and read an e-text of the introduction to book III of Spenser's *The Faerie Queene.*
   a. Find this e-text online at http://www.luminarium.org/renascence-editions/fqintro.html or https://scholarsbank.uoregon.edu/xmlui/handle/1794/784, both accessible formerly through links for online pages at the *Spenser Online* featured website cited above.

    b. Identify what the young Britomart saw one day in the mirror in her father's room.

    c. Why is this mirror unusual? Why did her father have it? Where did he get it?

    d. Why did Britomart go to a cave? What did she discover there?

    e. What reason did Britomart give for a journey she went on after these happenings?

    f. Note: Include quotes in your answers.

    g. Hint: See book III, part 2, verses 3, 7, 8, and 17 through 26.

4. Find and read the introductory verses of the e-texts of book II, book IV (also sometimes identified as Book IIII), book V, and book VI of Spenser's *The Faerie Queene*.

    a. Find this e-text online at http://www.luminarium.org/renascence-editions/fqintro.html or https://scholarsbank.uoregon.edu/xmlui/handle/1794/784, both accessible formerly through links for online pages at the *Spenser Online* featured website cited above.

    b. Identify each book and its character that portrays Justice, Friendship, Courtesy, and Temperance, citing each one's early English spelling.

    c. Quoting from the verses, identify a feature of each of these virtues and the character who is its personification.

5. Find and read an e-text of the *Faerie Queene*, book II, canto ix, on a castle called *The House of Temperance*.

    a. Find this e-text online at http://www.luminarium.org/renascence-editions/fqintro.html or https://scholarsbank.uoregon.edu/xmlui/handle/1794/784, both accessible formerly through links for online pages at the *Spenser Online* featured website cited above.

    b. Identify what the castle represents. What are some features of the castle's structure?

    c. What are two types of things the crowd of people at the castle's entrance represent?

    d. What do the three rooms in the castle's tower represent?

    e. Who are the people in those castle rooms? What do they do?

    f. Hint: Note verses 1 and 10, last part of verse 44 and so on to end of canto ix.

6. Spenser's *Faerie Queene* has been called an allegory with sub-allegories.

    a. Find e-text definitions of allegory; some connected to the *Faerie Queene*, at the websites http://www.bartleby.com/213/1112.html, http://www.shmoop.com/faerie-queene/allegory-symbol.html, https://prezi.com/9jhbrcyfzak2/literary-devices-of-the-faerie-queene, http://www.jstor.org/stable/27702688?seq=1#page_scan_tab_contents, plus critical analysis pages at www.bartleby.com found via resources page link at http://www.luminarium.org/renlit/spenlink.htm.

b. What are an allegory's features?

c. How is the *Faerie Queene*, book I an allegory; does it have sub-allegories? Quote examples.

d. Find other literary devices (e.g., other than allegory, Spenser stanza, Spenserian sonnet) in *The Faerie Queene*. See definitions at www.poetry foundation.org/learning/glossary-terms?category=techniques-and-fig ures-of-speech and devices Spenser used described at www.theartsjournal .org/index.php/site/article/download/126/123 and https://orangemanor .wordpress.com/2010/08/12/spenser%E2%80%94the-faerie-queene.

e. Write an essay in which you define three other literary devices (e.g., irony, ambiguity, epic, imitation, eclogue, pastoral) and how they appear in Spenser works. Give Spenser quotes.

7. Find and read e-texts of comments on Spenser by scholars through time.

a. Note for example: *Spenser As a Word Painter and Metrical Musician* and *Poetry of Spenser, Its Design* by Courthope at www.bartleby .com/213; George Saintsbury's *Spenser's Mission* at http://www .bartleby.com/213/1311.html; *Spenser's Narrative Imagery: Visual Structure of The Faerie Queene* by Josephine McMurtry via www .luminarium.org/renlit/spenseressay.htm. "In his charming introduction to Spenser . . . C. S. Lewis describes three ways to begin one's acquaintance with *Faerie Queene*" at www.catholiceducation.org/en/culture/ art/reading-the-classics-with-c-s-lewis.html; *C. S. Lewis on Spenser's Faerie Queene* at http://badgermum.blogspot.com/2014/05/c-s-lewis -on-spensers-faerie-queene.html; C.S. Lewis on Spenser in *Studies in Medieval and Renaissance Literature* (1966) after a book title search, then search inside the book for Spenser, at www.amazon.com including page 146, then see https://medievalmvb.wordpress.com/2014/06/18/ reading-c-s-lewis-on-spensers-use-of-allegory-in-the-faery-queene; Woolway's *Spenser and the Culture of Place* at https://extra.shu.ac.uk/ emls/iemls/conf/texts/woolway.html and at http://web.archive.org/ web/20010522163346/, http://www.dbu.edu/mitchell/spenserl.htm see *Spenser's Didactic Purpose in Book One of THE FAERIE QUEENE*, plus more critical essays on *The Faerie Queene* at www.lumina rium.org/renlit/spenseressay.htm, *Critics on Spenser's Style* at http:// web.archive.org/web/20030220153900/http://www.dbu.edu/mitch ell/spensers.htm, and http://www.enotes.com/topics/faerie-queene/ critical-essays.

b. Choose and identify three scholars' viewpoints.

c. Write an essay in which you suggest how these scholars' viewpoints help you understand Spenser's works. Quote from Spenser's and these scholars' works.

8. Find and read an e-text of the first verse, then the introductory verse, of the e-text of canto VI of Spenser's *Cantos of Mutabilitie*.
   a. Find links to e-texts of these *Cantos of Mutabilitie* below the *Faerie Queene* Cantos at http://www.luminarium.org/renascence-editions/fqintro.html or https://scholarsbank.uoregon.edu/xmlui/handle/1794/784, both accessible formerly through links for online pages at the *Spenser Online* featured website cited above.
   b. Quote from these e-text excerpts as you identify what Spenser meant by Mutabilitie.
   c. Provide one of Spenser's examples (from any of the other verses in Canto VI) of what he was writing about.
   d. Suggest your own example.
   e. Why do you think your example fits what Spenser wrote about?
9. Find and read e-texts of two of Edmund Spenser's *Complaints*, such as those titled *Visions of the Worlds Vanities and The Ruines of Time*.
   a. Find these e-texts at http://www.luminarium.org/renascence-editions/complaints.html and https://scholarsbank.uoregon.edu/xmlui/handle/1794/813, available formerly through the link for online pages at the Spenser Online featured website cited above.
   b. Identify, as you quote from each *Complaint*, how Spenser defined what each poem's title suggests.
   c. Include one example for each one that he provided.
   d. Suggest your own examples, one for each *Complaint*, that you think of from today's world and that you believe aptly exemplifies the definitions he provided.
   e. Keep d) just above in mind. Why do you think so?
10. Find and read an e-text of the introduction, plus the e-texts for April, October, and December, of Edmund Spenser's *The Shepheardes Calendar*.
    a. Find these e-texts at http://www.luminarium.org/renascence-editions/shepheard.html and https://scholarsbank.uoregon.edu/xmlui/handle/1794/833, both available formerly through the online pages link at the *Spenser Online* featured website.
    b. Identify, while including quotations, what Spenser referred to in the Introduction.
    c. Who and what are important in Spenser's April passages from the *Shepheardes Calendar*?
    d. What did Spenser define, and how, in the October passages from the *Calendar*?
    e. What did Spenser refer to in the December passages of the *Calendar*?

11. Edmund Spenser created a sonnet format now known as the Spenserian Sonnet.

   a. Find descriptions of the Spenserian Sonnet online at the *Sonnet Central* featured website at http://www.sonnets.org/basicforms.htm and http://www.sonnets.org/glossary.htm#195 then at http://www.literarydevices.com/sonnet.

   b. What are the Spenserian sonnet's features?

   c. See e-text samples online of this sonnet format in Spenser's sonnets, such as "Most Happy Letters (Amoretti LXXIV)," "One Day I Wrote Her Name (Amoretti LXXV)," found online at the featured websites http://www.literarydevices.com/sonnet, http://www.sanjeev.net/poetry/spenser-edmund/index.html, http://rpo.library.utoronto.ca/poets/spenser-edmund, http://www.poetryfoundation.org/bio/edmund-spenser, www.sonnets.org/spenser.htm, and http://www.webexhibits.org/poetry/explore_famous_sonnet_examples.html.

   d. Suggest how the Spenserian sonnet format's features help to bring out the theme in one of these Spenserian sonnets.

   e. Hints: As you work with these poems, note in the first poem what he wrote about the written word and how he described (together and individually) three women who had the same name and how they were important to him in different ways; in the second poem, identify what he tried to do, what thwarted him, what a woman said to him about what he was doing, and how he strongly defended his action.

12. Keep in mind what you did for question/activity 11 above.

   a. Study first two lines of e-texts of "Most Happy Letters" and line 10 from that poem, then, from "One Day I Wrote Her Name," second part of line 10 and all of line 11.

   b. Applying ideas that Spenser suggested in these lines, write two sonnets either on yourself and your life, or to someone else and that person's life.

   c. Note: You may replace "name" with any appropriate word when following what was written in the first poem.

13. Spenser wrote another form of poetry now named for him: the Spenserian Stanza.

   a. Find definitions and examples from Spenser's works online at the featured websites, http://andromeda.rutgers.edu/~jlynch/Terms/spenserian.html for Jack Lynch's *Guide to Literary Terms*, and Emory University's *A Handbook of Terms for Discussing Poetry* at http://www.english.emory.edu/classes/Handbook/Spenserian.html, and an introduction at http://www.gutenberg.org/files/15272/15272-h/15272-h.htm#Intro_III.4.

b. Identify the Spenserian Stanza's features.

c. To show your understanding of this poetic form, quote from the examples provided at the websites, or from other examples among e-texts of his works you can find online.

d. Write a poem on any subject in the style of the Spenserian Stanza.

14. Think of the language of Spenser's works. It is an early, but readable, form of English that is similar to, yet different from, modern English. Reading an original early English version of a Spenser story can be confusing, unless one has a glossary of early English words, reading guides, line-by-line translations, and/or parts in translation side by side, with early and modern English versions, or retellings in modern English.

a. Look at the http://spenserians.cath.vt.edu/TextRecord.php?textsid= 34525 website with an authoritative e-text of a late sixteenth-century version of *The Faerie Queene* with modernized spelling of early English words plus explanatory notes beside original English text. See https://en.wikisource.org/wiki/The_Faerie_Queene/Book_I/Glossary and use it with the www.luminarium.org/renascence-editions/fqintro .html or https://scholarsbank.uoregon.edu/xmlui/handle/1794/784 featured e-texts. Scroll to modern English words in right margin at http://anthony.sogang.ac.kr/books/Ren3.htm; see some retellings at www.gutenberg.org/files/41350/41350-h/41350-h.htm and at www. sacred-texts.com/neu/eng/sfq; and read the e-text article on *How to Read The Faerie Queene* at www.english.cam.ac.uk/spenseronline/ review/item/44.3.56.

b. Read book I, canto 1, verse i, of *Faerie Queene*, starting "A gentle knight. . . ."

c. Write an essay. Suggest how unfamiliar words you've found modern English words for, in glossaries or retellings or translations, enrich your reading of Spenser.

Additional websites for chapter 8 with more data to note

- https://clynjohnson.wordpress.com
  ○ click link to "Discovering English Literature . . . Additional Web Sites," then link to a wordpress.com blog at netedbooks, or go directly to http:// www.netedbooks.wordpress.com/home.

SIXTEENTH AND SEVENTEENTH CENTURIES—DRAMA

Chapter 9

Selections from Shakespeare's Plays

The Comedies

On the pages of the Massachusetts Institute of Technology website, the first featured site, see the first e-texts of *The Complete Works of Shakespeare*, including his plays in categories that identify the types of plays (i.e., Comedy, History, and Tragedy) as first done in 1623.

Under Comedy, see links to e-texts of the plays alphabetically (e.g., *All's Well That Ends Well*, *Cymbeline*, *Measure for Measure*, *A Midsummer Night's Dream*, *Much Ado About Nothing*, *The Tempest*, *Twelfth Night*, and *The Winter's Tale*).

Click a title link to go to links to acts and scenes of each comedy.

At the *Shakesper.net* featured website, note Scholarly Resources, links under Launching Points, BlogRoll, Life, Globe, Pedagogical, Research Sites, Concordances, Journals, and more.

At the *BardWebNet Shakespeare Resource Center* featured website, note links to Shakespearean Study, SRC Features, Reading List, Other Links, plus Reading Guide.

Note also quotes from Shakespeare's works at the *Great Books Online* Bartleby web pages.

Shakespearean critical analyses by well-known and lesser-known historical and modern critics and writers shed light on Shakespeare and his works, especially the comedies, ranging from critics Samuel Johnson and Samuel Taylor Coleridge to T. S. Eliot, and more.

FEATURED WEBSITES

- http://shakespeare.mit.edu/works.html
  - See links to e-texts in first column.
- http://www.rsc.org.uk/shakespeare/shakespeares-plays

- Click the play title photos to guides.
- See links to criticism at http://www.touchstone.bham.ac.uk/links/Criti cism.html such as *Shakespeare and His Critics* (1959).
- Or go directly to https://ia902707.us.archive.org/17/items/shakespear eandhi030042mbp/shakespeareandhi030042mbp.pdf and note a list of critics and where they are quoted in the book's text.
- Note also https://en.wikipedia.org/wiki/Timeline_of_Shakespeare_criti cism, at http://internetshakespeare.uvic.ca click Library, then *Shakespeare and the Classical Tradition*, then Facsimile Viewer, then title page image, then right arrow to go to page 3 where introduction starts.
- Note Samuel Johnson's 1765 *Preface to Shakespeare* at https://ebooks .adelaide.edu.au/j/johnson/samuel/preface/complete.html#preface.
- www.bardweb.net (click *SRC Features, Other Links*, and more).
  - See *Shakespeare Source Materials* at http://www.bardweb.net/content /ac/sources.html and http://www.bardweb.net/content/ac/shakesreader .html.
- At http://shaksper.net under *Scholarly Resources*, click *Shakespeare on the Internet*
- See Shakespeare works' quotes at http://www.bardwords.org, www.bar tleby.com/100/pages/page42.html, and www.infoplease.com/spot/shake spearequotes2.html.

DISCUSSION QUESTIONS AND ACTIVITIES

1. Shakespeare wrote of disguised characters and characters whose fates were not known to other characters although there were connections between these characters.
   a. Study e-texts of his comedies found online as cited in the featured website, http://shakespeare.mit.edu/works.html (click links).
   b. Identify one disguised character and one character with a fate unknown to others and the comedy or comedies in which they appear.
   c. Tell why a disguised character disguised oneself, how situations work out, and how Shakespeare used the technique well to tell the tale.
   d. Tell how a character got into a situation with her or his fate being unknown, how the character's fate becomes known, and how connected characters' stories work out well by this technique.
2. Read an e-text of Shakespeare's comedy *As You Like It*, noting act 2, scene 7, found online through featured website pagehttp://shakespeare. mit.edu/asyoulikeit/index.html.
   a. Scroll to the last quarter of the page to see the character Jacques's speech that begins "All the world's a stage."

b. Write a paragraph identifying, while using quotations, what Shakespeare or his character said are the seven ages of man.

c. Write another paragraph. Suggest other ages of humankind that Shakespeare's character did not mention, or other types of people he could have mentioned in the ages of life that he did mention.

d. Write a poem with stanzas featuring different ages of, or times in, human beings' lives.

3. Study Shakespeare's plays that are comedies whose e-text versions are found online at the featured website, http://shakespeare.mit.edu/works .html (click links).

a. Think about the comedy plays' women characters.

b. Write an essay. Compare two or three women in the same Shakespearean comedy. Note their traits and, if applicable, how they interact with one another or other characters.

c. Write another essay. Compare two or three women characters from different comedies.

d. Note, compare, their traits. How do they interact with other characters?

4. Study Shakespeare's plays that are comedies whose e-texts are found online at the featured website http://shakespeare.mit.edu/works.html (click links).

a. Note interactions between sisters, brothers, sisters and brothers, and cousins.

b. Choose examples from the comedies for each of the four groups.

c. Identify each character in each group and the plays in which they appear.

d. Comment on these characters' relationships with one another.

e. Hint for d) just above: include how each helps or hinders the other, or, if trouble exists between them, how they work it out.

5. Study Shakespeare's comedies whose e-text versions are found online at the featured website, http://shakespeare.mit.edu/works.html (click links).

a. Note happenings between daughters or sons and their fathers or mothers.

b. Choose examples of, and describe, three such situations from three different comedies.

c. How are problems solved between a parent and a child or children?

d. Note relationships in *The Tempest, The Winter's Tale, As You Like It, Cymbeline*, or other comedies.

6. Read online quotations or excerpts on birds, other animals, flowers, other plants, or nature during the seasons, from Shakespeare's comedies.

a. Find these quotations online at https://archive.org/details/birdsof shakespea00geikuoft, http://cwf-fcf.org/en/discover-wildlife/resources/ online-articles/the-bards-birds.html?referrer=https://www.google.com,

http://www.shakespeare-online.com/quotes/shakespeareonflowers
.html, https://www.questia.com/library/journal/1G1-162353983/theory
-from-the-fringes-animals-ecocriticism-shakespeare websites, and
1871 James Edmund Harting's *The Birds of Shakespeare Critically
Examined, Explained, and Illustrated,* http://books.google.com.

   b. Write an essay. Quote four phrases from each category from different
      Shakespearean comedies as you suggest what each phrase refers to in
      a play.
   c. Tell what the phrases mean to you.
   d. Tip: Select a quote from *As You Like It.*

7. Find e-texts of famous quotations or passages from Shakespeare's plays
   that are comedies, especially e-texts whose first lines or beginning phrases
   are listed just below.
   a. Find these quotations online at the www.bartleby.com/100/pages/
      page42.html featured website and by titles and themes at www.shake
      speare-online.com/quotes, plus at www.enotes.com/shakespeare-quotes.
   b. Find, read, and comment on quotes beginning with "We are such stuff,"
      "Be not afraid of," "Our remedies," "The quality of mercy," and another
      one of your choice.
   c. Hints: Identify the comedy in which a quote appears. How is a quote
      meaningful as part of that play, and apart from the play (e.g., to anyone
      at any time in the past or present, to today's world or someone in it, or
      to you)? Suggest each quote's meaning for Shakespeare and to his time.
   d. Tip: For help with part of c) above, see http://www.shakespear
      estudyguide.com (note links under Shakespeare's Life and Times), and
      see real and fictional Shakespearean places at http://www.shakespeare-
      online.com/plays/playsettings.html, http://www.bbc.com/news/uk-eng
      land-coventry-warwickshire-27041828, and http://www.britainexpress
      .com/attraction-tags.htm?tag=William+Shakespeare.

8. Keep in mind what you did for question 7 above.
   a. Choose six other e-texts of quotes from six of Shakespeare's plays that
      are comedies.
   b. Find quotes of *Bartlett's Familiar Shakespeare Quotations* at www
      .bartleby.com/100/pages/page42.html and http://www.bardwords.org
      featured websites, plus at http://www.shakespeare-online.com/quotes,
      www.enotes.com/shakespeare-quotes, and www.infoplease.com/spot/
      shakespearequotes2.html.
   c. Explain why you chose each quote, then follow hints and tip in ques-
      tion 7 above.

9. Read e-texts of monologues by women and men in Shakespeare's plays
   that are comedies.
   a. Find these e-texts by browsing the www.shakespeare-monologues
      .org/home website.

b. Choose a monologue for a woman, then follow hints and tip in question 7 above to your chosen monologue quote.

c. Choose a monologue for a man, then follow hints and tip in question 7 above to your chosen monologue quote.

d. Read e-text of *"Men vs. Women: Examining the Relationship between Genre and Gender in Shakespeare?"* (2002?) by Kristen Kurzawski, found online at http://teachers.yale.edu/curriculum/viewer/initiative_08.01.01_u.

e. Why does Ms Kurzawski claim that gender and genre determine portrayals in the plays?

f. Give examples from one or two of Shakespearean comedies that you find online and that have portrayals of women and men as Ms. Kurzawski suggests.

10. Find and read an e-text of the article *Critical Approaches to Shakespeare: Some Initial Observations* (2001) by Ian Johnston.

a. Find this e-text online at http://records.viu.ca/~johnstoi/eng366/approaches.htm.

b. Identify four approaches and "other interpretative approaches" to Shakespeare's works, then quote from or refer to the article as you explain each approach briefly.

c. Choose examples from Shakespeare's comedies for each approach you discovered above. Explain how each example fits with one or the other of Johnston's approaches.

d. Tip: Include quotations from the plays and the article.

11. Find and read e-texts of three classic essays on Shakespeare from literary history and written by British or American critics (e.g., Samuel Johnson, Samuel Taylor Coleridge, T. S. Eliot, Edward Dowden, William Hazlitt, Aldous Huxley, Ralph Waldo Emerson, Mark Twain).

a. Find e-texts of essays (some as featured sites above and some as additional sites below). See overviews at https://en.wikipedia.org/wiki/Timeline_of_Shakespeare_criticism and Shakespearean critics quoted in http://www.touchstone.bham.ac.uk/links/Criticism.html. Note in particular T. S. Eliot's early and later views of Shakespeare commented on at http://www.jstor.org/stable/23094254?seq=1#page_scan_tab_contents in *T. S. Eliot and Shakespeare* (1967) by Philip L. Marcus, with excerpts from Eliot on Shakespeare quoted by David Galison www.huffingtonpost.com/david-galenson/recognizing-that-poets-do_b_3479117.html in 2013 and in "Comedy as . . ." (1976) and *Twelfth Night* on page 132, number 1161 in *De Shakespeare A T. S. Eliot* by Henri Fluchere with title search at http://books.google.com for *Comedy, An Annotated Bibliography* by James E. Evans, and Eliot in his *The Use of Poetry and the Use of Criticism* found after book title search at http://books.google.com plus a subject search in book for Shakespeare, criticism, imagination and *Midsummer Night's Dream*, plus objective correlative. Note also *Preface to Shakespeare* (1765) by Samuel Johnson with *Measure for Measure* notes at https://ebooks.adelaide.edu.au/j/johnson/samuel/preface/complete.html#preface, and Coleridge's *Essays on Shakespeare* (1907) at https://ia802303.us.archive.org/0/items/coleridgesessays00cole/coleridgesessays00cole_bw.pdf. See *Shakespeare, or The Poet* by Emerson (1904) at www.bartleby.com/90/0405.html, Twain's *Is Shakespeare Dead?* (1909) at http://web.archive.org/web/20090711002917/http://etext.lib.virginia.edu/toc/modeng/public/TwaDead.html (click links, e.g., for chapter 7); Hazlett's *Characters of Shakespeare* (1916) at http://www.saylor.org/site/wp- content/uploads/2011/01/CHARACTERS-OF-SHAKESPEARE.pdf; Dowden's 1875 "But Shakespeare possessed . . ." on page six and following pages of *Shakespeare: His Mind and Art* at http://assets.cambridge.org/97811080/00765/excerpt/9781108000765_excerpt.pdf; "Consider Shakespeare's achievement as a dramatist" (1965) by Huxley at www.sirbacon.org/links/huxley2.htm (for this comment, scroll to phrases in paragraph three's second part) (scroll down for more data, excerpts from the history plays, e.g., "Henry V"); note also Dowden's 1893 *Introduction to Shakespeare* after title search at http://books.google.com and search inside for comedies; and *Twelfth Night* in Patricia W. Greene's "Shakespeare's Clowns" at http://www.uh.edu/honors/Programs-Minors/honors-and-the-schools/houston-teachers-institute/curriculum-units/pdfs/2009/shakespeare/green-09-shakespeare.pdf.

b. Identify a main point in each chosen essay; one that is an essay writer's view, and one that is another essay writer's view, of Shakespeare and his comedies.

c. Quote quotations from one comedy or a few comedies as examples to show that you understand main points of what the critics wrote.

12. Read online definitions of the present and from the past to discover the precise meanings of comedy, dramatic comedy, tragic comedy, and tragedy.

a. Find definitions at http://www.siue.edu/~ejoy/eng208NotesOnComedyAndTragedy.htm with Ian Johnston's *Dramatic Structure: Comedy and Tragedy, and Shakespeare* (n.d.).

b. Write an essay identifying exactly each definition and what it means, how meanings have changed through literary history, or how some basic features have stayed the same.

c. Choose one type of comedy, dramatic comedy, or tragic comedy.

d. Select a Shakespeare comedy that you think fits the type of comedy you chose in c).

e. Find this comedy online as cited in a featured website's url and sites summary above.

f. Write an essay. Explain, with examples and quotes from the play, and a definition, why this play is the particular type of comedy chosen above.

13. Phrases from Shakespeare's works, including some from his comedies, have often been quoted in television episodes, movies, and books of *Star Trek* (the popular science fiction media franchise of modern times).

a. Visit and study websites with data and quotes on Shakespeare and *Star Trek* such as http://englishscholar.com/shakespeare_startrek.htm (see quotes from television episodes, movies, and novels connected to *Star Trek*), see links to *To Bardly Go, The Hollywood Bard*, and more at http://shakespeareonline.freeservers.com/toc.html. See e-texts of comedies you find online through other sites cited in this chapter and see http://memory-alpha.org/wiki/William_Shakespeare *Star Trek's MemoryAlpha Library.*

b. Choose a phrase from one of Shakespeare's comedies (e.g., *The Tempest* and *As You Like It*) that is quoted in something of *Star Trek*. Identify the Shakespeare comedy and a *Star Trek* episode, movie, or book where the quote appears, and the character or characters who spoke the quote.

c. Suggest why these particular Shakespearean words fit well with this *Star Trek* story.

d. Explain why you think Shakespeare's comedies, a particular Shakespearean comedy, and certain words, plus *Star Trek* work well together.

14. Find and study web pages at sites that feature something about literature derived from Shakespeare's works, including his comedies.

a. Find and study web pages such as http://www.barbarapaul.com/shake.html (note titles), http://www.shakespeare-online.com/biography/shakespearewriter.html (note influence on writers), and note data on, e.g., titles taken from Shakespeare's comedies.

b. Choose three literary works at these websites, then identify something in each that is based on something in one of the Shakespearean comedies.

c. Hint: Think of Shakespeare titles and familiar quotations.

d. Write a story title, and a play scene, neither related, but based on phrases you choose from one of Shakespeare's comedy titles, excerpts, or quotes, found online at http://shakespeare.mit.edu/works.html, http://www.bardwords.org, www.bartleby.com/100/pages/page 42.html, and www.infoplease.com/spot/shakespearequotes2.html featured websites, or a) sites above.

15. Think of the interesting idea that many codes or ciphers may be hidden in Shakespeare's works as some scholars and respected authors believe, then look at the comedies that have a code or cipher.

    a. To find out about types of codes or ciphers and their features that may be found in Shakespeare's works in general, and then in the comedies in particular, see websites such as http://www.wondersandmarvels .com/2012/12/shakespeares-secrets-a-hidden-cipher-in-literatures -greatest-works.html, http://www.rictin.com/codes-in-shakespeare, www.theguardian.com/uk/2005/aug/28/arts.books, and http://shake spearethehiddentruth.com (click "film trailer").

    b. Identify some codes or cyphers that scholars have discovered in Shakespeare works. Note especially those that suggest hidden messages in the plays in general, and the comedies in particular. See something at the end of *All's Well That Ends Well*, and some things in *Much Ado About Nothing*, *The Merry Wives of Windsor*, and *The Tempest*.

    c. Write an essay. With quotations or specific facts, suggest how one or another of these codes may enrich your study of the plays in general, and the comedies in particular.

    d. Identify what some scholars suggest are in the codes or ciphers which anticipate something well-known in today's world. Suggest its significance.

    e. Hints: a code or cipher may refer to the actual author of Shakespeare's works, something about a hidden prince, something about Sir Francis Bacon, something about a hidden treasure, or various messages (some political or religious or something else).

Additional websites for chapter 9 with more data to note

- https://clynjohnson.wordpress.com
  - click link to "Discovering English Literature . . . Additional Web Sites," then link to a wordpress.com blog at netedbooks), or go directly to http:// www.netedbooks.wordpress.com/home.

Chapter 10

Selections from Shakespeare's Plays

The Histories

An area of the Massachusetts Institute of Technology website features the first e-texts of "The Complete Works of Shakespeare," including the plays. Title links of the plays are listed alphabetically under categories identifying types of plays, including history, tragedy, and comedy.

Under History, note the plays *Henry IV* (parts 1 and 2), *Henry V*, *Henry VI* (parts 1, 2, and 3), *Henry VIII*, *King John*, *Richard II*, and *Richard III*. After clicking a title link, note links to acts and scenes and the titles of each.

Note the Royal Shakespeare Company featured website's guide to Shakespeare's plays with introductions, quotations, educational tips, and more.

At the Internet Shakespeare Editions website's Resources area, click Critical Materials (check boxes for introductions, critical surveys, essays; choose items on plays from a list).

At Shakespeare Navigators site, find links to annotated texts, and quotes by or about.

Note also features of *BardWeb*, sites with Shakespearean Monologues, influence of Shakespeare on other writers, *Star Trek*, plus characters in the plays and codes in the plays.

FEATURED WEBSITES

- http://shakespeare.mit.edu/works.html
- Note links to e-texts in second column.http://www.backstage.com/mono logues/shakespeare,http://www.acting-school-stop.com/shakespeare-monologues.html

- www.rsc.org.uk/shakespeare/shakespeares-plays
  - Click play title photos for guides.
- http://internetshakespeare.uvic.ca/Foyer
  - Click resources at top right, critical materials.
  - http://records.viu.ca/~johnstoi/eng366/approaches.htm, http://records. viu.ca/~johnstoi/eng366/interpretation.htm, of Shakespeare's histories at https://ebooks.adelaide.edu.au/c/coleridge/samuel_taylor/shakespeare-ben-jonson-beaumont-and-fletcher/chapter27.html; http://www.shake speare-online.com/scholars.
- http://www.shakespeare-navigators.com
  - Click title links to find quotes from plays.
  - http://www.william-shakespeare.info/william-shakespeare-quotes.htm; see quotes about Shakespeare from Elizabeth Barrett Browning to T. S. Eliot at http://www.shakespeare-online.com/quotes/themanquotes.html.
  - www.bardweb.net (click resources link to go to page of links to sites with more data)
  - http://shaksper.net/scholarly-resources/shakespeare-on-the-internet (click site name links to sites with additional information)
  - https://en.wikipedia.org/wiki/List_of_titles_of_works_taken_from _Shakespeare,
  - Shakespeare's Influence on Other Artists at http://www.shakespeare-online.com/biography/shakespearewriter.html,
- Titles Inspired by Shakespeare Phrases at http://mentalfloss.com/ article/61142/13-titles-inspired-shakespeare-phrases, www.barbarapaul.com/ shake.html.
- Click play titles to Titles from Shakespeare or go to http://webcache. googleusercontent.com/search?q=cache:http://www.barbarapaul.com/ shake.html&num=1&strip=0&vwsrc=0).
- www.opensourceshakespeare.org/views/plays/characters/chardisplay.php
  - Click links to sources for characters' speeches, www.shakespeare-online .com/plays.
  - Click titles, follow links to plays, and articles on characters, at www.nos weatshakespeare.com/characters
  - https://en.wikipedia.org/wiki/List_of_Shakespearean_characters_(A-K)
  - https://en.wikipedia.org/wiki/List_of_Shakespearean_characters_(L-Z),
  - http://www.saylor.org/site/wp-content/uploads/2011/01/CHARAC-TERS-OF-SHAKESPEARE.pdf; http://www.shakespeare-online.com/ plays/characters
- www.summituniversitypress.com/chapters/Shakespeare-Code-sample .pdf

DISCUSSION QUESTIONS AND ACTIVITIES

1. Read an e-text of Shakespeare's history play *King Henry IV* at a featured website.
   a. Find the e-text online at http://shakespeare.mit.edu/works.html via column two.
   b. Describe young Prince Hal's character. Feature how, and why, he changes as the play progresses. With your explanation, include quotes by Hal and other characters.
   c. Hint: As part of your description and explanation, feature quotations of what he says in part I, act 1, scene 2, and part II, act 5.
2. Read an e-text of a scene in the Duke of York's Garden in Shakespeare's history play *Richard II* (i.e., act 3, scene 4).
   a. Find e-text online at http://shakespeare.mit.edu/works.html featured site via column two.
   b. How does the gardener, his assistant, compare natural things in the garden to political situations?
   c. Tell what the gardener does after the queen overhears the gardener and the gardener's assistant and he tells her of the happenings on which his comparisons are based.
3. Study some young people and children represented in e-texts of Shakespeare's history plays.
   a. Find these e-texts online at the http://shakespeare.mit.edu/works.html featured website in column 2; and in articles' e-texts, such as Portrayals of Children in Shakespeare's Plays at www.lotsofessays.com/view paper/1711985.html, in Shakespeare and Childhood at http://ebooks .cambridge.org/chapter.jsf?bid=CBO9780511483493&cid=CBO978 0511483493A015 see excerpt of A. J. Piesse's Character Building: Shakespeare's Children in Context, page 64; https://www.aca demia.edu/2403589/Radmila_Nasti%C4%87_The_Child_as_Other_in _Shakespeares_Plays (see some types of children in Shakespeare's works); see Child Characters in Shakespeare . . . at http://gradworks .umi.com/34/16/3416909.html.
   b. Write an essay. Identify how Shakespeare wrote of young people, children in his plays.
   c. Write an essay in which you compare and contrast two young characters in the history plays. They may appear on stage and speak or not, or be referred to with suggestions of what's happening with them off stage.

    d. Study, for example, young Prince Hal in *King Henry IV*, young Arthur in King John, the two young Princes in *Richard III*, or others you discover.

    e. Compare some young people in other Shakespearean plays, one a comedy and one a tragedy, but not those considered in d) just above. Study, Miranda in *The Tempest*, Cordelia in *King Lear*, young Macduff in *Macbeth*, act IV, scene 2.

4. Study e-texts of Shakespeare's plays that are histories and e-texts of articles for those plays, then investigate women characters in the plays.

    a. Find e-texts of the plays that are histories in second column at the featured website http://shakespeare.mit.edu/works.html and find data on the Women in Shakespeare as cited in the plays, through the websites www.nosweatshakespeare.com/characters, http://www.shakespeareswords.com/Special-Features-Female-Characters, http://www.beta-iatefl.org/861/blog-publications/women-in-shakespeare, http://shakespeare.about.com/od/criticalapproaches/a/intro_women.htm, http://shakespeare.about.com/od/criticalapproaches/a/types_women.htm.

    b. Write an essay. Compare traits and experiences of two or more women in the same play.

    c. For b) just above, write about Katherine of Aragon/Anne Bullen in King Henry VIII, or Elinor/Constance in *King John* and Calpurnia/Portia in *Julius Caesar*.

    d. Write another essay. Identify how scholars see Shakespeare's portrayals of women and their traits in Shakespeare's history plays.

5. Read an e-text of the 2001 article "Studies in Shakespeare: Critical Approaches to Shakespeare: Some Initial Observations" by Ian Johnston.

    a. Find this article's e-text online at http://records.viu.ca/~johnstoi/eng366/approaches.htm.

    b. Identify four approaches and "other interpretative approaches" to Shakespeare's works.

    c. Explain each approach briefly as you refer to Johnston's article.

    d. For each, choose examples from history plays (e.g., *Richard II & III* and *Henry IV*).

    e. Explain how each Shakespearean example fits one or the other of Johnston's approaches.

    f. Also check Johnston's article "Studies in Shakespeare: On Scholarship and Literary Interpretation" (2005) at http://records.viu.ca/~johnstoi/eng366/interpretation.htm.

6. Read e-texts of two classic critical analysis essays on Shakespeare from literary history and written by British or American critics.

    a. Find e-texts of critical analyses by classic author/scholar/critics such as Samuel Johnson, John Dryden, T. S. Eliot, plus Ralph Waldo Emerson;

along with Samuel Taylor Coleridge, Edward Dowden, William Hazlitt, Aldous Huxley, Mark Twain, and others.

b. Find these e-texts online separately or collected. See featured and additional websites, including an overview of noted and lesser-known Shakespearean scholar-critics and their works at http://www .shakespeare-online.com/scholars plus excerpts from some of their works via http://books.google.com or www.amazon.com or elsewhere on the web after Google search or via http://www.shakespeare-online .com or at http://www.bardweb.net/content/index.html. Note too Samuel Johnson on Shakespeare's histories at https://ebooks.adelaide .edu.au/c/coleridge/samuel_taylor/shakespeare-ben-jonson-beaumont-and-fletcher/chapter27.html; comments on early and later views of Shakespeare by T. S. Eliot in Eliot's "Search for the Transcendent in Late Shakespeare" on page 111 of John Freeh's *Shakespeare's Last Plays* (2002) at http://books.google.com, and www.jstor.org/ stable/23094254?seq=1#page_scan_tab_contents, and comment on Shakespearean style at https://www.academia.edu/22844804/What _is_the_Objective_Correlative; comments by Emerson at http://www .bartleby.com/90/0405.html, Coleridge at https://archive.org/details/ coleridgesessays00cole, and more.

c. Read and identify some main points in Johnson's and Eliot's comments, using quotes.

d. Select another two essays with comments by a British and an American author/critic, read these essays and identify their main points, including quotations.

e. As you research, write, note essay writers' views of Shakespeare, his history plays.

f. Write an essay in which you quote examples from the history plays' e-texts and the critics' essays as you aim to illustrate how you understand some of the critics' writings.

7. Find and read some monologues by women and monologues by men in Shakespeare's plays, especially the history plays.

a. Find monologues online at http://www.stagemilk.com/male-shake speare-monologues, http://www.shakespeare-monologues.org/women, http://www.bottletreeinc.com/teen_monologues_shakespeare.html, http://www.acting-school-stop.com/shakespeare-monologues.html, http://www.backstage.com/monologues/shakespeare.

b. Choose a monologue for a woman. Adapt and apply the hints in question 8 below to this chosen quoted monologue.

c. Choose a monologue for a man. Adapt and apply the hints in question 8 below to this chosen quoted monologue.

8. Find e-texts of famous passages in Shakespeare's history plays.
   a. Choose, from *Richard III*; Henry IV, part 2, act 3, scene 1 and two passages from *Henry IV*, part 2, act 4, scene 5.
   b. See first lines in Shakespearean sentences at c) below; then see phrases from the plays at www.bartleby.com/100/pages/page42.html; also see http://www.bbc.co.uk/schools/teachers/offbyheart/speeches, http://theshakespeareblog.com/2011/05/greatest-shakespeare-speeches, http://www.nosweatshakespeare.com/quotes/famous-shakespeare-quotes, and http://gwydir.demon.co.uk/jo/quotes/speech.htm.
   c. Find, read, and comment on, passages beginning "Now is the winter of our discontent," "So wise, so young," "Uneasy lies the head that wears a crown," "O coward conscience," "A horse! A horse!" "O dear father . . . my due from thee . . .," "my most inward true and duteous nature Teacheth . . ."; and another passage you choose.
   d. Write an essay in which you suggest how a quote is meaningful as part of a play where it is found, as via links at http://www.bartleby.com/100/138.html.
   e. Suggest also how a quote is meaningful apart from the play (e.g., to anyone at anytime in the past or present, to today's world or someone in it, or to your life).
   f. Suggest how each quote fits Shakespeare and his time.
   g. For some help with last parts, see Shakespeare's Life, Time, and Places at www.stratford-upon-avon.co.uk/wslife.htm, see www.britannia.com/hiddenlondon/shakespeare.html (click links), www.bardweb.net/england.html (see overview, then click links).
   h. For help understanding phrases, see modern translations, at http://nfs.sparknotes.com, http://nfs.sparknotes.com/henry4pt2/page_481.html (click title; select act, scene, phrase; see original and modern translations); see www.nosweatshakespeare.com/shakespeares-plays/modern-english-translations; see scholars' modern translations such as act 2, scene 2 spoken by Flavius in the Kenneth Cavander translation of Shakespeare's *Timon of Athens*.
9. Keep in mind question/activity 8 above.
   a. Choose six other e-text quotations from Shakespeare's history plays.
   b. Find online through www.william-shakespeare.info/william-shakespeare-quotes.htm or www.shakespeare-navigators.com or other Shakespeare quotation sites on nature.
   c. Explain why you chose each quote. Tell what's important to you about each one.
   d. Follow activities d) through f) in question 8 above.
10. Find and browse the "Shakespeare and Classic *Star Trek*" web document.
   a. Find it at http://englishscholar.com/shakespeare_startrek.htm, see also http://memory-alpha.org/wiki/William_Shakespeare, and find other

Shakespeare and *Star Trek* sites cited in the additional websites whose link is cited below. Note also *Star Trek* episode guides at http://www.tv.com/shows/star-trek/episodes.

b. Check the e-texts of Shakespeare's histories found online in this chapter and find something from a Shakespeare history that is quoted in something of *Star Trek*.

c. Identify a history play and a *Star Trek* title from a television episode, movie, or book, and characters (from *Star Trek* and from Shakespeare's history) who spoke the quote.

d. Suggest why these Shakespearean words fit well with this *Star Trek* story, and why Shakespeare's histories and *Star Trek* work well together.

11. Study web pages about literature inspired by Shakespeare's works.

a. Find these pages online at the featured sites http://www.barbara-paul.com/shake.html, http://mentalfloss.com/article/61142/13-titles-inspired-shakespeare-phrases, https://en.wikipedia.org/wiki/List_of_titles_of_works_taken_from_Shakespeare; and at additional sites such as Aldous Huxley's A Sentence From Shakespeare (1944) at http://www.sirbacon.org/links/huxley1.htm), Shakespeare's Influence on Other Artists at http://www.shakespeare-online.com/biography/shakespearewriter.html, and www.bbc.co.uk/drama/shakespeare/60secondshakespeare/teachers_themes_list.shtml.

b. Choose six literary works' titles, three from different sites.

c. Identify something in each work that is based on one of Shakespeare's history plays.

d. Hint for c) just above: Think of his titles and quotations.

e. Write your own story title and a play scene based on two phrases you choose from any of Shakespeare's history plays' titles, quotations or excerpts at a featured website or at websites referred to in the first part of this question/activity.

f. Tip for e) just above: Your story title and play scene do not have to be connected.

12. Read an e-text of Shakespeare's history play *Henry V*; noting especially act 4, scene 1.

a. Note that this part of the play is where young King Henry (the former Prince Hal) disguises himself and walks among his soldiers in their camp one night before a battle.

b. Find this e-text at http://shakespeare.mit.edu/henryv/henryv.4.1.html featured site page.

c. Write an essay in which you suggest why he disguised himself, what he discovered, and why it was important that he did it.

   d. Hints: What happened during talks with the characters Pistol and
      Michael Williams? What are some things Henry says near the end of
      the scene when alone, after soldiers exited, then after the character
      Erpingham exited?
13. Find and read some web documents whose author/scholars claim that
    since Shakespeare's time there is a hidden code or codes hiding in Shake-
    speare's works.
   a. Find e-texts of documents at the www.summituniversitypress.com/
      chapters/Shakespeare-Code-sample.pdf featured site, http://www
      .wondersandmarvels.com/2012/12/shakespeares-secrets-a-hidden-
      cipher-in-literatures-greatest-works.html (the first and last para-
      graphs), http://www.theguardian.com/uk/2005/aug/28/arts.books and
      other additional sites.
   b. Write an essay. Quote from these documents and from Shakespeare's
      works, especially the histories, to reveal what codes may be hidden
      among Shakespeare's words.
   c. Hints: Consider references to a forgotten prince, Shakespeare's time's
      politics and religious aspects hidden in the plays; plus how a code in
      the sonnets may be in the plays.

Additional websites for chapter 10 with more data to note

- https://clynjohnson.wordpress.com
  ○ Click link to "Discovering English Literature . . . Additional Web Sites,"
    then link to a wordpress.com blog at netedbooks), or go directly to http://
    www.netedbooks.wordpress.com/home.

Chapter 11

Selections from Shakespeare's Plays

The Tragedies

On the first featured site, an area of the Massachusetts Institute of Technology website, note the first e-texts of *The Complete Works of Shakespeare*, including his dramatic works, written by this foremost British writer who lived from 1564 until 1616.

Title links of the plays are listed under tragedy, history, and comedy.

Under "Tragedy," see tragedies listed alphabetically, including *Hamlet, King Lear, Macbeth, Romeo and Juliet,* as well as historical tragedies such as *Julius Caesar, Antony and Cleopatra,* and more, with dates based on times of performance or publication.

Click a title link, note links to acts and scenes and the titles of each tragedy, plus links in e-texts to definitions of unfamiliar words.

At the Royal Shakespeare Company site, click title photo links to find data on each play, with quotes, key words and facts, and tips for educators.

At BardNet, note links to plays, SRC features, Shakespeare Study, and Other Links.

At *Shakespeare on the Internet*, see links to Research Sites and Scholarly Resources (e.g., "Library of Essays," Pedagogy—Teaching Resources, Cook's Tour of Internet Resources for Students and Scholars, and more) on the author, his works, his life and times.

Note *Shakespeare and His Critics, Earlier Critics' Extracts*, Jonson, Eliot, Oates, and Ian Johnston at http://people.brandeis.edu/~teuber/earlycrit.html, www.celestialtimepiece.com, https://shine.unibas.ch/linkscriticismrec.htm, a *Shakespeare Blog*, and more.

FEATURED WEBSITES

- http://shakespeare.mit.edu/works.html
  - Click title links in the third column.
- http://www.rsc.org.uk/shakespeare/shakespeares-plays
  - Click the play title photo to see links to synopsis, and information for teachers.
  - www.bardweb.net; http://shaksper.net under *Scholarly Resources* click *Shakespeare on the Internet* link.
  - See Shakespeare's critics at https://archive.org/details/shakespeare andhi030042mbp.
  - See more critics at https://web.archive.org/web/20131006112331/http:// shakespeare.palomar.edu/playcriticism.htm, http://theshakespeareblog .com/2014/01/t-s-eliot-and-shakespeare, https://shine.unibas.ch/links criticismrec.htm.
  - See Ben Jonson on Shakespeare at https://www.nytimes.com/ books/00/02/13/bookend/bookend.html, http://www.luminarium.org/ sevenlit/jonson/benshake.htm, http://www.shmoop.com/to-the-memory-of-my-beloved, http://www.sourcetext.com/greenwood/jands/02.htm, and poem at https://www.poetryfoundation.org/poems-and-poets/poems/ detail/44466, plus https://andromeda.rutgers.edu/~jlynch/Texts/pope-shakespeare.html, https://www.oneeyedman.net/school-archive/classes/ fulltext/www.mala.bc.ca/~johnstoi/eng366/approaches.htm.

DISCUSSION QUESTIONS AND ACTIVITIES

1. Read web definitions of tragedy and Shakespeare's dramas.
   a. Find these definitions by searching featured sites such as http://shak sper.net/scholarly-resources/shakespeare-on-the-internet and www .bardweb.net, plus sites found through the additional websites link cited below.
   b. Keep in mind a definition you found as you select an e-text of one of the tragic plays found online at the featured MIT website, http://shake speare.mit.edu/works.html.
   c. Including quotes from the chosen play, and a definition, write an essay. Suggest how that play and its main character(s) are expressions and examples of that definition.
2. Study excerpts on particular subjects or symbols in Shakespeare's tragic plays' e-texts.
   a. Find these e-texts online at featured website http://shakespeare.mit .edu/works.html and at additional websites via link below, then online

under subjects such as birds and plants and note *Shake Sphere—A Comprehensive Shakespeare Study Guide* online at http://www.shake spearestudyguide.com and in the additional websites cited below.

b. Identify references to, flowers, birds, the sun, and stars, and then suggest their significance in the story and about the characters.

c. Note, Romeo and Juliet, act two, scenes 2 and 3; act 3, scene 5, and act 4, scene 5; *Hamlet*, the Ophelia and flowers scenes in act 4, scene 5, and act 4, scene 7; *Macbeth*, act 4, scene 1; *Othello*, act 1, scene 3.

3. Study an e-text of Shakespeare's tragic play *King Lear*.

   a. Find it online at the featured website's page, http://shakespeare.mit .edu/lear/index.html.

   b. What is significant about the storm in act 3?

   c. Identify some plant metaphors and how or why are they important in, act 2, scene 3, and act 4, scenes 4 and 6?

   d. Identify some animal metaphors and how or why they are important in, act 1, scene 4, act 3, scene 4, and act 5, scene 2.

   e. Identify the fool and his importance, especially in act 1, scene 4.

   f. Identify similarities and differences between the characters King Lear/ Gloucester, Cordelia/Edgar, the fool/Edgar, Albany/Edgar, Edmund/ Regan/Goneril.

   g. See also question 8 below, noting characters Cleopatra, Antony, and Enobarbus.

4. Study the e-text of Shakespeare's tragic play *Romeo and Juliet*.

   a. Find it online at featured website page, http://shakespeare.mit.edu/ romeo_juliet/index.html.

   b. See Friar Lawrence's comments in act 2, scene 3. What does the friar think of Romeo; yet why does he agree to perform the marriage ceremony for Romeo and Juliet?

   c. See act 5, scene 3. How is Friar Lawrence's goal (one he had in mind when he agreed to marry Romeo and Juliet) achieved, but not in the way he had hoped it would be?

5. Study an e-text of Shakespeare's tragic play *Hamlet*.

   a. Find it online at featured website's page, http://shakespeare.mit.edu/ hamlet/index.html.

   b. Identify why Hamlet returns home from a university, and what he finds out from his friend Horatio. Who does he see and what is he told?

   c. How does Hamlet begin his plan to prove what he was told? How does he expose the guilty person and make him pay for what he has done?

   d. Who are Gertrude, Ophelia, Polonius, Laertes, and Fortinbras?

   e. What connection and importance does each character in c) above have to Hamlet?

    f. What unexpectedly happens to each character cited above as a consequence of Hamlet's actions, by accident, or because of the guilty person?

6. Study an e-text of Shakespeare's tragic play *Macbeth*.
    a. Find it online at featured the website's page, http://shakespeare.mit.edu/macbeth/index.html.
    b. Identify what three witches tell Macbeth and Banquo.
    c. When does Macbeth start to believe them?
    d. What do Macbeth and his wife decide to do, and why, because of what the witches said?
    e. How do Lady Macbeth and Macbeth psychologically act in different ways before and after they do what they decide to do?
    f. What other things does Macbeth feel compelled to do after he and his wife carry out their first plan?
    g. Which two statements do the witches make when Macbeth sees them again? Why do these statements make him think he is safe from consequences for his actions, yet why are his assumptions not true?

7. Study an e-text of Shakespeare's tragic play *Julius Caesar*.
    a. Find online at featured website page, http://shakespeare.mit.edu/julius_caesar/index.html.
    b. What is a soothsayer's warning to Julius Caesar during a procession praising Caesar for winning a war?
    c. What does Calpurnia (Caesar's wife) see in a dream? How is it connected to what the soothsayer said?
    d. Who are the men who decide that Caesar must be assassinated? Why do they think he should be assassinated?
    e. Why does Caesar's friend Brutus decide to be one of the assassins?
    f. How does Antony react to the assassins at first? What does he say to the crowd of citizens?
    g. How do the citizens react to the assassins because of what Antony says to them?
    h. What do the citizens cause the assassins to do?
    i. What strange things are experienced by the two main assassins, Cassius and Brutus? What do they argue about as they prepare for war with Antony, Octavian and Lepidus, who have taken over ruling Rome?
    j. What happens to the two main assassins? How do Antony and Octavian react to what happened to Brutus?

8. Study an e-text of Shakespeare's tragic play *Antony and Cleopatra*.
    a. Find it online at the featured website page, http://shakespeare.mit.edu/cleopatra/index.html.
    b. How well is Antony ruling Rome with Octavian and Lepidus as the play opens?

    c. How is Cleopatra described by Philo and Demetrius in act 1, scene one, and by Enobarbus in act 2, scene 2, each with reference to Antony?

    d. Why did Antony first go to Egypt? Why did he stay there, and then why did he go back to Rome? What causes him to return to Egypt?

    e. How does Cleopatra with her fleet of ships cause trouble for Antony?

    f. Tell about Enobarbus (a main soldier of Antony's forces). Suggest why he may be thought of as an important although minor character.

    g. In addition to Enobarbus in the play, see commentaries about him online through the additional websites link cited below.

    h. Why and how do Antony and Cleopatra die? How does Octavian treat them before and after their deaths?

9. Study an e-text of Shakespeare's tragic play *Othello.*

    a. Find it online at the featured website's page, http://shakespeare.mit .edu/othello/index.html.

    b. Why does Desdemona choose to marry Othello?

    c. What did Desdemona's father believe was the reason that made her marry Othello?

    d. Who are Iago, Rodrigo, and Cassio? What does each do to cause Othello to mistrust, then murder, his wife? How is a handkerchief important to what happens? What happened to Othello, Cassio, Iago, and Rodrigo, after the murder?

10. Keep in mind Shakespeare's women characters as you read e-texts of some of his tragic plays, or excerpts, found online at the featured site, http://shakespeare.mit.edu/works.html.

    a. Write an essay comparing and contrasting traits of two or more women in the same tragedy (e.g., the three sisters in *King Lear*). Include quotes on why two sisters are thought of as better daughters during the play, and which sister is later found to be the better daughter? Explain why.

    b. Write another essay comparing and contrasting traits of two or more women not in the same play (e.g., Ophelia or Gertrude from "*Hamlet*," Juliet from *Romeo and Juliet*, Lady Macbeth or witches from *Macbeth*, Desdemona from *Othello*, Cleopatra from *Antony and Cleopatra*), or others you have read about.

11. Read e-texts of *Monologues by Women and Men* in Shakespeare's tragic plays.

    a. Find these e-texts by searching a *Shakespeare's Monologues* website, found at www.shakespeare-monologues.org.

    b. Choose a monologue for a woman with phrases starting "Oh what a noble mind" by Ophelia in *Hamlet* or "O Romeo" by Juliet in *Romeo and Juliet*, or another one from another tragic Shakespearean play.

   c. Adapt and apply question 12's hints below to chosen woman's mono-
      logue quote.
   d. Choose a monologue for a man, such as Hamlet's "To be or not to
      be," or Romeo's "But soft, what light," or Antony's "Friends, Romans,
      Countrymen" in *Julius Caesar* or another one from another tragic
      Shakespearean play.
   e. Adapt and apply question 12's hints below to the chosen man's mono-
      logue quote.
12. Find and read e-texts of famous passages in Shakespeare's tragic plays
    (e.g., e-texts with first lines or beginning phrases listed in a) below and
    found at the *Shakespeare Quotes* at www.enotes.com/shakespeare-quotes
    or http://www.enotes.com/shakespeare-quotes/index, or other quotation
    sites found through the *William Shakespeare on the Internet* and *BardWeb*
    featured websites, or at *Additional Websites* whose link is cited below.
   a. Select, read, and comment on six passages, choosing from among
      passages that begin "The play's the thing," "The fault, dear Brutus,"
      "Tomorrow, and tomorrow," "What a piece of work is a man," "There
      are more things in heaven and earth," "To Sleep, Perchance to Dream,"
      "What's in a Name?"
   b. Hints: How is a quote meaningful for the play it is in?
   c. How is a quote meaningful apart from a play (e.g., to anyone, any
      time, past or present, to your life, or to today's world)?
   d. How does each quote fit Shakespeare and his time?
   e. Tip: For help, see http://www.rsc.org.uk/shakespeares-life-and-times;
      http://shakespeare-gesellschaft.de/en/info/faqs/shakespeare/shake
      speares-times.html; *Shakespeare's Life and Times* at "Annie's Page"
      at www.reocities.com/Athens/Oracle/3221/shakespeare.html; sites
      found through *William Shakespeare on the Internet*, or through addi-
      tional websites found through a link below.
13. Keep in mind question/activity 12 above.
   a. Choose six other e-text quotes from Shakespeare's plays, especially
      the tragedies, one each as found at the websites cited in b) just below.
   b. Visit websites on Shakespeare's works (e.g., *Shakespeare Online*
      sites; *Resources at the Shakespeare Society Online*; *Quotes from the
      Works of Shakespeare*; Shakespeare in *Bartlett's Familiar Quotations,
      Quotations About Flowers or Plants, Birds or Other Animals, Nature
      During the Seasons*; Selected Quotes from Shakespeare's Tragedies),
      or others, found online at *Additional Websites* cited below, at *William
      Shakespeare on the Internet*, or *BardWeb*, or in other chapters in ser. 1
      vol. 1.
   c. Explain why you chose each quote.
   d. Tip: Follow hints and tip in question/activity 12 above.

14. Choose and read e-texts of two classic essays from literary history on Shakespeare, written by past and recent British and American critics or other critics in English.

   a. Choose from among the critics Ben Jonson, Samuel Johnson, S. T. Coleridge, Edward Dowden, William Hazlitt, Aldous Huxley, Ralph Waldo Emerson, Mark Twain, T. S. Eliot, Joyce Carol Oates, Anna Jameson, and Bianca-Oana Petrut.

   b. Of works of authors cited in a) above, find e-texts online individually, or at *Extracts from Earlier Critics (1710–1945)* at http://people .brandeis.edu/~teuber/earlycrit.html, or at *Shakespeare on the Internet* or *BardWeb* featured sites cited above, or at *Shakespeare Online* or *Shakespeare Resources* websites, found online via additional websites that feature e-texts of critical analysis articles.

   c. Identify one main point in each essay, with the points referring to each writer's view of Shakespeare and his works, emphasizing the tragic plays.

   d. Find and quote quotes from Shakespeare's tragic plays to show your understanding of what the critics wrote.

   e. Tip: Give quotes from plays different from what the critics quoted.

15. Read an e-text of *Critical Approaches to Shakespeare: Some Initial Observations* (2001) by Ian Johnston.

   a. Find it online at https://www.oneeyedman.net/school-archive/classes/ fulltext/www.mala.bc.ca/~johnstoi/eng366/approaches.htm, cited as a featured website above and noted in question/activity 14 above.

   b. Identify four approaches and "some other interpretative approaches" to Shakespeare's works. Explain each approach briefly. Be sure to cite or refer to phrases in the article.

   c. For each approach cited above, choose an example you see from a featured website's tragic plays by Shakespeare. Explain how each example fits with one or the other of Johnston's approaches.

16. Visit websites found through searches at the *William Shakespeare on the Internet* or *BardWeb* featured sites or via sites found through additional websites link cited below.

   a. Find, read, and note definitions of dreams, astronomy and cosmology, astrology and alchemy, ghosts and apparitions, and magic, and Shakespeare's uses of them in his tragic plays.

   b. Select five examples from the tragedies, one for each subject referred to just above.

   c. Quote from definitions and plays as you explain how your examples show each subject's importance in a tragedy.

   d. Compare his uses of topics in a tragedy and in other play types (e.g., history, comedy).

    e. Tip: Find Shakespeare's history and comic plays online as cited in this book's (series 01 volume 01) chapters on his histories and comedies.

17. Find and study websites with Shakespeare spin-offs, parodies, other versions, and phrases.

    a. Look for *Shakespeare Spinoffs and Parodies* and *List of Titles of Works Based on Shakespearean Phrases*.

    b. Find these websites through the *Shakespeare on the Internet* or *Bard-Web* featured websites cited above, or at suggested additional websites for which there is a link below.

    c. Choose three literary works in which you see and then identify something based on one of Shakespeare's tragedies. Hint: Think of his titles and quotations.

    d. Write your own story title, and play scene, based on two phrases you choose from any tragic play title, quotes or excerpts, you find at websites referred to at the beginning of this Question/Activity. Note: story title, play scene, need not be connected.

Additional websites for chapter 11 with more data to note

- https://clynjohnson.wordpress.com
  - Click the link to "*Discovering English Literature . . .*" *Miscellany*, then link to a wordpress.com page at netedbooks on *Additional Websites*, or go directly to http://netedbooks.wordpress.com/home.

Section IV

SEVENTEENTH CENTURY—POETRY

Chapter 12

Excerpts from *The Passionate Pilgrim, Sonnets to Sundry Notes of Music, "The Phoenix and the Turtle"*

See featured websites/pages on Shakespeare, his poetry, and poems in his plays. Start with the *Complete Works of William Shakespeare* links page found at the *Bartleby: Great Books Online* website. Scroll to and click Poetry Index of First Lines link or Poetry Contents link to go to pages that feature links to poems other than the well-known sonnets.

Among these pages of e-texts of poems written by, or attributed to, William Shakespeare, see links to first lines of the fourteen parts of *The Passionate Pilgrim* (1599), and first lines of the six *Sonnets to Sundry Notes of Music* (1599) (where sundry meaning is diverse). See also links to *The Phoenix and Turtle [Dove]* (1601), and *Venus and Adonis* (1593).

First reproduced online in 2000, these poems are from *The Oxford Shakespeare Version of 1914*, in an early form of English in which his sonnets, other poems, were originally written.

At the University of Ontario's *Representative Poetry Online*, see notes after poem's e-texts and more classic analyses by Coleridge, Twain, Emerson, and Edward Dowden. See also modern commentaries on *Rise of Poetic Interpretation in Shakespeare* at Google Books, the Poetry Foundation's editorial by Monroe, and Johnston's *Critical Approaches to Shakespeare*.

Note also the *Shakespeare As Poet and Dramatist* website, the analysis "The Making of Shakespeare's Dramatic Poetry" at the *Project Muse* website, *Observations on Shakespeare's Dramatic Poetry* by Johnston, plus poetry in the plays as cited at the *See What Is There, The Wandering Hermit,* and *No Sweat Shakespeare* sites, plus analyses at the *pbs.org* site, and more.

FEATURED WEBSITES

- www.bartleby.com/70
  - Scroll to, click, Poetry—Index of First Lines link, then first line links; or click Poetry—Contents then links to poems by title).
  - Click links to e-texts of poems with notes about them at http://rpo.library .utoronto.ca/poets/shakespeare-william.
- See commentaries on the poetry at www.britannica.com/biography/ William-Shakespeare/Literary-criticism.
  - See the annotated list at https://en.wikipedia.org/wiki/Timeline_of _Shakespeare_criticism
  - See Edward Dowden at http://search.eb.com/shakespeare/article-9031083, http://www.poetryfoundation.org/features/articles/detail/89184.
  - Click X at top of page for big print of seven pages of *Poetry Magazine* founder Harriet Monroe's comments, 2001 lectures, http://records.viu .ca/~johnstoi/eng366/lectures/lectures.htm including *Critical Approaches to Shakespeare* and *Observations on Shakespeare's Dramatic Poetry.*
- See at http://search.eb.com/shakespeare/article-232442 *Shakespeare as Poet and Dramatist.*
  - at http://thewanderinghermit.com/x-poetry/plays.htm poems in the plays, http://www.nosweatshakespeare.com/resources/shakespeare-puns,
  - http://www.seewhatisthere.com/poetry-shake.html, plus analyses of poems in the plays in "The Rise of Poetic Interpretation in Shakespeare" in *The Shakespeare Play As Poem* after book title search at http://books .google.com.
  - At www.pbs.org/standarddeviantstv/transcript_shakespeare.html Click link to Shake*speare's Use of Language*, *The Importance of Words.*
  - See a review on *Making of Shakespeare's Dramatic Poetry,* https://muse .jhu.edu/article/514275/pdf.
- See Shakespeare quotes at http://www.seewhatisthere.com/poetry-shake -misc.html, http://absoluteshakespeare.com/trivia/quotes/quotes.htm.
- Click links by theme subject or play title at http://www.shakespeare-online .com/quotes.

DISCUSSION QUESTIONS AND ACTIVITIES

1. Find and read an e-text of "If Music and Sweet Poetry Agree," a part of Shakespeare's poem *The Passionate Pilgrim.*
   a. Find this e-text at the featured website's page, http://www.bartleby .com/70/5208.html.

b. Note the beginning of the poem.

c. What is suggested in a statement that you can identify by the words "if" and "then"?

d. Identify some examples Shakespeare gave to support his viewpoint.

e. What did he conclude?

f. What did he say about poets as he aimed to back up his claim?

2. Find and read e-texts of *Sonnets to Sundry Notes of Music* such as "As It Fell Upon A Day."

   a. Find this e-text at the featured website's page, http://www.bartleby .com/70/536.html.

   b. Quoting some phrases as examples, identify what is merry about a month in spring, especially with reference to nature.

   c. Which bird is not quite merry, why, and how does it show its mood?

   d. What does the narrator think about because of the bird? What does he say to the bird?

   e. Explain the difference between fellow creatures or people who seem to be friends and those who really are friends.

   f. How does one's environment seem to react to one's situation?

   g. Which natural feature does the narrator compare with words? Do you agree or not? Why?

   h. Provide your own examples as you write a poem on a subject you find in this poem.

   i. Maybe write your poem in the form of a sonnet (defined at http://web .cn.edu/kwheeler/lit_terms_S.html).

3. Find and read an e-text of Shakespeare's poem *The Phoenix and the Turtle [Dove]*.

   a. Find this e-text at the featured website's page, http://www.bartleby .com/70/54.html.

   b. Study lines 25 through 27, 29, 30, 33 through 36, 37 through 39, 41 and 42.

   c. Identify, with quotes, examples of a relationship between the two birds, then suggest how one or more examples may represent a relationship between two people.

   d. Tip: See notes at *Representative Poetry Online* featured website's page, http://rpo.library.utoronto.ca/poems/phoenix-and-turtle.

4. Look further at Shakespeare's poem "The Phoenix and the Turtle [Dove]," whose e-text is found online at the featured website's page, http://www .bartleby.com/70/54.html.

   a. Note especially the poem's beginning verses.

   b. Study the descriptions of birds that, as the narrator comments, came to commemorate the lives and relationship of the phoenix and the turtledove.

c. Identify what the two commemorated birds represent in general.

d. Identify the other birds at, or trying to come to, the commemoration.

e. Why was each bird allowed at the commemoration, or not?

f. Provide brief descriptions.

g. Tip: See notes at *Representative Poetry Online* featured website's page, http://rpo.library.utoronto.ca/poems/phoenix-and-turtle.

5. Study again Shakespeare's poem "The Phoenix and the Turtle [Dove]," whose e-text is found at the featured website's page http://www.bartleby .com/70/54.html.

a. Note that this poem has been called an allegory.

b. Search for, and read about, this literary term at the *Literary Vocabulary* website: http://web.cn.edu/kwheeler/lit_terms_A.html.

c. Write an essay in which you suggest how this poem is an allegory.

6. Find e-texts of poems in Shakespeare's plays, choose one to study, and analyze it.

a. Find some of Shakespeare's poems in his plays at the featured sites, http://thewanderinghermit.com/x-poetry/plays.htm, http://www .nosweatshakespeare.com/resources/shakespeare-puns, and at http:// www.seewhatisthere.com/poetry-shake.html.

b. Find analyses of poems in the plays at www.pbs.org/standarddeviant stv/transcript_shakespeare.html (click link to *Shakespeare's Use of Language, The Importance of Words,* etc.), in "The Rise of Poetic Inter- pretation in Shakespeare" in *The Shakespeare Play As Poem* (1980) by S. Viswanathan after book title search at http://books.google.com, Hal- liday's *The Poetry of Shakespeare's Plays* at http://books.google.com, review of G. R. Hubbard's *The Making of Shakespeare's Dramatic Poetry* at https://muse.jhu.edu/article/514275/pdf.

c. Find e-texts of the plays in which the poems appear at http:// shakespeare.mit.edu, noting Shakespeare's Comedies, Histories, and Tragedies.

d. Write an essay. Identify poetic features in the plays as critics cited above point out.

e. Find examples of poems in the plays as critics define poetry in the plays.

f. Explain, as you see it, a chosen poem's importance in its play.

g. How may this poem be important outside of the play (i.e., in his time, and in today's world, in your life, or for people of any time and place)?

h. Tip: In your comments, include a poem's theme and how it applies to its play, then as it,

7. Visit websites with Shakespearean quotations.

a. Visit, for example, http://www.seewhatisthere.com/poetry-shake-misc. html, http://absoluteshakespeare.com/trivia/quotes/quotes.htm, and click links by theme subject or play title at http://www.shakespeare-online.com/quotes.

b. Search for quotations from Shakespeare's poems.

c. Choose a quotation, by subject if possible.

d. What is the quotation's main point?

e. Suggest what the poem means to you.

8. Find and read two e-texts, one classic essay and one recent noteworthy essay on Shakespeare.

a. Keep in mind the comment that Shakespeare is "the greatest poet of modern times and . . . of all time" as stated by South American scholar Otto Carpeaux at https://en.wikipedia.org/wiki/Timeline_of_Shakespeare_criticism#Twentieth_century.

b. See e-texts of essays written by British and American critics and writers of the past such as Samuel Taylor Coleridge, Ralph Waldo Emerson, Mark Twain, Edward Dowden, and more. See documents by modern critics such as Harriet Monroe and Ian Johnston; others cited at www.britannica.com/biography/William-Shakespeare/Literary-criticism with links to more data, including some on the bard's dramatic poetry, poems, and sonnets.

c. Find essays' e-texts at www.pagebypagebooks.com/Mark_Twain/Is_Shakespeare_Dead, https://archive.org/details/coleridgesessays00cole, www.bartleby.com/90/0405.html, plus at http://records.viu.ca/~johnstoi/eng366/lectures/lectures.htm, a review at G. R. Hibbard's *Making of Shakespeare's Dramatic Poetry* at https://muse.jhu.edu/article/514275/pdf, an annotated list at https://en.wikipedia.org/wiki/Timeline_of_Shakespeare_criticism, and a bibliography at http://shaksper.net/archive/1990/27-september/80-basic-shakespearean-criticism-145.

d. Identify from each essay's main points that refer to the essay writers' views of Shakespeare and his works, especially his poems or poetry in the plays.

e. Quote a sentence or two from these essays. Be sure the quotes feature main points.

f. Find and quote quotations from Shakespeare's poems at the featured websites, http://www.seewhatisthere.com/poetry-shake-misc.html, http://absoluteshakespeare.com/trivia/quotes/quotes.htm, and click links by theme, subject, or play title at http://www.shakespeare-online.com/quotes, then suggest how these quotes from the poems are examples of the critics' main points.

g. After identifying main points in the two essays you chose, write a paragraph in which you comment on how these essay points help you understand how Shakespeare and his poems can express a meaning of a quote that Carpeaux commented on, stated in question 8a just above, with title search of *William Shakespeare* by Wikipedians, and scroll to page 124.

Additional websites for chapter 12, with more data to note

- https://clynjohnson.wordpress.com
  - Click *Discovering English Literature in Bits & Bytes*, then click link to *Additional Information* to go with chapters; or go directly to https://netedbooks.wordpress.com/home.

Chapter 13

Sonnets plus Dramatic Poetry by William Shakespeare

See e-texts of poems, especially sonnets and dramatic poetry, written by or attributed to William Shakespeare at each featured website.

See features of the *Folger Shakespeare Library Digital Texts* website, noting links to 144 sonnets. On the *Bartleby: The Great Books Online* website, click links to sonnets and other poems numbered I–CLIV (equal to 1–154). At both sites, see links to first lines, sonnet numbers.

Poems at the *Folger Digital Texts* site were placed online starting 2010 while poems at the *Bartleby* site, first appeared online in 2000, from "The Oxford Shakespeare" version of 1914, providing modern English translation of early English in which sonnets were originally written.

Note also searches by first line or well-known line at the *Rhyme Zone* website, and the *Shakespeare Online* site's quote page with links to Shakespeare passages via subject links.

Note websites on Shakespeare's dramatic poetry, such as Kim Ballard's *Prose and Verse in Shakespeare's Plays* at the *British Library* a review of *The Making of Shakespeare's Dramatic Poetry* by G. R. Hibbard (1981), and other sites with definitions and examples.

More websites provide insight into, and commentaries on, Shakespeare's sonnets. Note Coleridge's "Shakespeare, A Poet" in *Literary Remains of Shakespeare* (1819), "Sonnets" in Auden's *Lectures on Shakespeare* (2000), plus Ian Johnston's 1999 *A Look at Shakespeare's Sonnets*, Kenneth C. Bennett's 2007 *Threading Shakespeare's Sonnets*, data on *Shakespearean Sonnet Basics* and *How to Analyze a Shakespearean Sonnet*.

Note also more commentaries at sites cited in the additional websites linked below.

FEATURED WEBSITES

- http://www.folger.edu/sonnets
  - Click "read poems online in Folger Digital Texts."
  - Scroll poem links by numbers 1–144 with first lines near them.
  - See search area at right where searches by sonnet number, or text by first line, are possible, especially for sonnets 145–154.
  - See: www.bartleby.com/70/index1.html.
  - Click links to poems arranged by Roman numbers I–CLIV or first lines near them.
  - Do a popular word search at www.rhymezone.com/shakespeare or search by most popular lines to find passages from Shakespeare's sonnets and other works, www.shakespeares-sonnets.com/firstlines.php.
- See Shakespeare's Sonnets at www.bardweb.net/poetry.html#sonnets.
  - See *an Outline of the Contents of Shakespeare's Sonnets* by Raymond M. Alden at http://www.shakespeare-online.com/sonnets/sonnetgroup-analysis.html.
  - See another group analysis at http://www.handprint.com/SC/SHK/sonnets.html#synopsis.
- See modern and classic Shakespearean scholars at http://www.shakespeareis.com/interview-searches/the-interviews/scholars, http://web.archive.org/web/20101222063944, and /http:/records.viu.ca/~johnstoi/eng366/sonnets.htm.
  - Ian Johnston's 1999 article, "A Note on Shakespeare's Sonnets," Kenneth C. Bennett's *Threading Shakespeare's Sonnets* (2007) at http://campus.lakeforest.edu/kbennett/sonnets/entirebook.pdf.
  - Nigel Davies's *The Place 2 Be* at http://www.reocities.com/Athens/Troy/4081/Sonnets.html. Note criticism through time such as T. S. Eliot at the paragraph starting with "The only way" at www.bartleby.com/200/sw9.html.
  - See "Sonnets" in *Lectures on Shakespeare* (2000) by W. H. Auden as edited by Arthur Kirsh at *Lectures* title search at http://books.google.com.
  - See *Shakespeare as Poet* (with "first importance of a poet") by Ralph Waldo Emerson at www.bartleby.com/90/0405.html.
  - See "Shakespeare, a Poet" in *Literary Remains of Shakespeare* (1819) by Samuel Taylor Coleridge at www.gutenberg.org/cache/epub/8533/pg8533-images.html, www.pagebypagebooks.com/Mark_Twain/Is_Shakespeare_Dead (note chapters X and VIII), http://web.uvic.ca/~mbest1/engl366c/tn3.html with John Dryden's mixed review comments, and others' comments in *Additional Websites* cited below.
- www.shakespeare-online.com

- ○ Note *Why Study Shakespeare* and its links to *How to Analyze a Shakespearean Sonnet* and *Shakespearean Sonnet Basics*.
- ○ Kim Ballard's *Prose and Verse in Shakespeare's Plays* at *British Library* website: http://www.bl.uk/shakespeare/articles/prose-and-verse-in -shakespeares-plays.
- ○ See review of *The Making of Shakespeare's Dramatic Poetry* by G. R. Hibbard (1981) at http://muse.jhu.edu/article/514275.
- ○ See dramatic verse defined with Shakespeare notes at https://en.wikipedia .org/wiki/Verse_drama_and_dramatic_verse, http://study.com/acad emy/lesson/dramatic-poetry-definition-examples.html, http://hubpages .com/literature/dramatic-poetry/605, and http://oxfordindex.oup.com/ view/10.1093/oxfordhb/9780199607747.013.0024.
- • Quotations by themes at www.shakespeare-online.com/quotes.

DISCUSSION QUESTIONS AND ACTIVITIES

1. Read an e-text reproduction of William Shakespeare's sonnet 91 (91) (XCI) found at the featured websites and whose first line starts with *Some Glory In.*
   a. Find e-text at www.folger.edu/sonnets and www.bartleby.com/70/ index1.html sites.
   b. Identify five things that some people *glory in,* then *what every humor* (i.e., mood) *has,* and where it finds something (which you should identify) *above the rest.*
   c. Tell what *these particulars are not,* and what the narrator believes about *all these.* How?
   d. What is better than which four things and how (as adjectives indicate)?
   e. Of what does the narrator *boast,* yet what is he aware of that would be *wretched?*
2. Find and read an e-text reproduction of William Shakespeare's sonnet fifty-five (55) (LV), whose first line starts with *Not marble, nor. . . .*
   a. Find e-text at www.folger.edu/sonnets and www.bartleby.com/70/ index1.html sites.
   b. Scroll to and study the second part of line 2, all of line 3, lines 9 through 11, and the first and second parts of line 14.
   c. Identify what will cause something about a person to endure, noting four phrases for one way that the person will endure, and then two other phrases for two other ways.
   d. Scroll to and study line 1, the first part of line 2, and lines 4 through 7.

e. Quoting some phrases, identify two things that will not endure although something of the person will, and then note how that person will not be affected by those things.

f. Keep in mind critics have identified at least two features that make this poem important. Suggest what you think the two features are. Support your answer with quotes.

3. Study further the e-text reproduction of Shakespeare's sonnet number 55.

a. Find e-text at www.folger.edu/sonnets and www.bartleby.com/70/index1.htmlsites.

b. Scroll to and reread lines 4 through 8 especially.

c. Quote phrases from these lines as you write a poem (perhaps a sonnet) or an essay, applying them to today's world and to someone in it of the present or recent past.

4. Find and read an e-text of William Shakespeare's sonnet 29 (29) whose first line starts *When in disgrace with. . . .*

a. Find e-text at www.folger.edu/sonnets and www.bartleby.com/70/index1.html sites.

b. Scroll to and study lines 1 through 7.

c. Identify the narrator's present state of being.

d. Tell three things he does with relation to it.

e. Study line 8.

f. Suggest what is puzzling about its statement.

g. Study line 9.

h. What does the narrator think of himself in relation to what he wrote in the earlier lines?

i. Scroll to and study lines 10 through 14.

j. Why does the narrator change his mind? How does he compare himself to a particular bird? What does he scorn and why?

5. Find and read e-text reproductions of some other sonnets by William Shakespeare.

a. Find, those sonnets whose first lines and numbers are "Shall I Compare Thee to a Summer's Day" (18), That Time of Year Thou Mayst in Me Behold (73), "Like As the Waves Make Towards the Pebbled Shore" (60), "How Heavy Do I Journey on the Way" (50), "When to the Sessions of Sweet Silent Thought" (30), "Let Us Not to the Marriage of True Minds Admit Impediments" (116), and "Love is too young to know . . ." (151).

b. Find e-text at www.folger.edu/sonnets and www.bartleby.com/70/index1.html sites.

c. Choose three and identify (with quoted phrases) the main point of each.

    d. Quote more phrases from each sonnet to support the main point you see in each one.

6. While you keep in mind questions/activities 1 through 5 above, and William Shakespeare's sonnets online that they refer to, find and read Nigel Davies' e-text introduction to Shakespeare's sonnets.

    a. Find online as detailed in tips just below, selecting sonnets by subject or first line as listed on Davies's page at http://www.reocities.com/Athens/Troy/4081/Sonnets.html formerly found through link at the *Surfing With the Bard* website at www.shakespearehigh.com/library/surfbard/index.htm.

    b. Keep Davies's introduction in mind as you find, choose, and read e-text reproductions of some Shakespeare sonnets found at the featured *Folger* and *Bartleby* featured websites, and at the *Surfing With the Bard* website.

    c. Follow Davies's viewpoints as you analyze three Shakespeare sonnets you choose. Tell how he portrayed each one's theme as he followed or altered rules defining a sonnet.

    d. Tips: Select sonnets by subject or first line as listed on Davies's online page cited as stated in a) above. Note, for example, subjects such as advice to a young man, comments to a woman or about women, something about human nature, nature symbolizing or compared with human nature, time, poet and muse. See, for example, numbers 12, 14, 15, 17, 21, 33 through 35, 38, 36, and 65. One of the sonnets you choose can be one of the sonnets referred to in questions/activities 1 through 5 above.

7. Visit websites featuring e-texts of documents including *Outline of the Contents of Shakespeare's Sonnets* by Raymond M. Alden and *Quotations by Theme* at *Shakespeare Online*.

    a. Find these e-texts at featured websites including http://www.shakespeare-online.com/sonnets/sonnetgroupanalysis.html and http://www.shakespeare-online.com/quotes.

    b. Search for quotations by subject and the sonnets or other poems in which they appear.

    c. Find sonnet e-texts at www.folger.edu/sonnets and www.bartleby.com/70/index1.html sites.

    d. Identify the quotation's main point.

    e. Suggest what the sonnet means.

    f. Hint: Select a quote from a sonnet featuring a subject such as memory, or remembrance, perfection, praise, time, or something else.

8. Find and read e-text reproductions of some classic critical essays on Shakespeare and poetry.

a. Look for quotes from writings by noted British and American critics and writers of the nineteenth and twentieth centuries, such as Samuel Taylor Coleridge, Ralph Waldo Emerson, Mark Twain, W. H. Auden, and more.

b. Check featured websites for e-texts by John Dryden at http://web .uvic.ca/~mbest1/engl366c/tn3.html, Samuel Taylor Coleridge at www .gutenberg.org/cache/epub/8533/pg8533-images.html, Ralph Waldo Emerson at www.bartleby.com/90/0405.html, Samuel Clemens or Mark Twain at www.pagebypagebooks.com/Mark_Twain/Is_Shake speare_Dead, and T. S. Eliot at www.bartleby.com/200/sw9.html (scroll to paragraph starting "The only way").

c. Identify from each essay a main point referring to the essay writer's view of Shakespeare and his works, especially his sonnets plus his dramatic poetry and his other poems.

d. Quote a sentence or two featuring each essay's main point.

e. Find and quote quotations from Shakespeare's sonnets at a featured website cited above, then suggest how the quoted sonnets are examples of the critics' main points.

9. Find online definitions of dramatic verse and e-texts of examples in Shakespeare's plays.

a. Check e-text of Ballard's *Prose and Verse in Shakespeare's Plays* at http://www.bl.uk/shakespeare/articles/prose-and-verse-in-shake speares-plays, at http://muse.jhu.edu/article/514275 a review of *The Making of Shakespeare's Dramatic Poetry* by G. R. Hibbard, plus definitions at https://en.wikipedia.org/wiki/Verse_drama_and_dramatic _verse (with verse variations), plus at http://study.com/academy/lesson/ dramatic-poetry-definition-examples.html, verse and prose in Shake speare at http://shakespeare-w.com/english/shakespeare/terms.html.

b. Find e-texts of Shakespeare's dramatic verse in Ballard's article at *British Library* site, at the review of Hibbard's work at http://muse.jhu.edu/ article/514275, a definition at http://hubpages.com/literature/dramatic- poetry/605, and *Shakespeare's Dramatic Verse Line* at http://oxfordin dex.oup.com/view/10.1093/oxfordhb/9780199607747.013.0024.

c. Write an essay in which you list features and four types of verse, plus provide a definition of dramatic verse, then suggest, with quotation examples, how some of Shakespeare's works are examples of this literary form.

Additional websites for chapter 13 with more data

- https://clynjohnson.wordpress.com
  - Click link to *Discovering English Literature in Bits & Bytes . . . Additional Websites*, or go directly to https://www.netedbooks.worpress.com/home.

Chapter 14

Various Writings by John Donne

John Donne's writings, many complex, range from controversial romantic versifications, to poetry with metaphors from science and other subjects, plus works with religious overtones.

Some featured sites, including the *Luminarium*, show Donne sometimes writing in a short literary form (e.g., epigram), as in "An Obscure Writer," "Disinherited," and nearly twenty other titles.

Basic features and critical analyses of this format, defined by a variety of authors, include wit and conceit, both considered in various ways, often as written by metaphysical poets.

Note also the *Luminarium* and other websites with epigrammatic quotes from Donne's verse letters and other works.

The *Luminarium's* Donne articles area, and other featured websites of books online, including *Moulton's Library of Literary Criticism* volumes 1–4, *Digital Donne Variorum* and e-notes' annotated essays from *Early Modern Studies Journal* (e.g., "Use of Space") have analyses of Donne, his works, from his time to the present, with various views. See Donne in an epigram; Coleridge on Donne; T. S. Eliot noting Donne's traits; H. J. C. Grierson defining Donne and metaphysical poetry; plus other views of critics in modern times and critics from the recent past.

FEATURED WEBSITES

- http://www.gutenberg.org/files/48688/48688-h/48688-h.htm
  - ○ See area with Donne's epigrams in a 1912 publication.
- www.luminarium.org/sevenlit/donne/donnebib.htm
  - ○ See *Letters to Several Personages.*

- Note Donne's poems and first lines listed as verse letters or parts of them at http://books.wwnorton.com/books/webad.aspx?id=10135.
- http://www.luminarium.org/sevenlit/donne/donnequotes.htm
- See commentaries on Donne and his works, at *Moulton's Library of Literary Criticism* at http://www.oocities.org/litpageplus/donnmoul.html.
  - See *Oxford Handbook of John Donne,* https://www.amazon.co.uk ed. by M. Thomas Hester, others, pages 1, 99, 105.
  - www.luminarium.org/sevenlit/donne/donnessays.htm including Sparkes' . . . *the Use of Geometric Conceits in the Poetic Works of Donne* . . ., and Morgan's *Donne and the Tradition of English Literature*, www.humanitiesweb .org/spa/lcl/ID/42, four annotated bibliographies at http://donnevariorum .tamu.edu/html/resources/index.html.
  - Click links to volumes in pdf format by the years 1912–1967, 1968–1978, 1979–1996, and 1997–2008.
  - See http://www.enotes.com/topics/john-donne/critical-essays/donne-john #critical-essays-donne-john-criticism
  - Click links to e-texts of articles from literary magazines.
  - See an excerpt from a preview of article on modern views of Donne's poems, by Helen Gardner; plus introduction and commentary to vol. 2 of *Poems of John Donne* edited by Grierson in 1912 at https://catalog .hathitrust.org/Record/001017306 (click vol. 2 link, scroll to areas).
  - http://neoenglishsystem.blogspot.com/2010/11/conceits-and-images-of -john-donne.html, scroll to sources section and its comment by Joan Bennett, literary critic.

DISCUSSION QUESTIONS AND ACTIVITIES

1. Find online the phrases Samuel Taylor Coleridge used to define "What Is an Epigram?"
   a. Find an e-text of this definition at https://www.poets.org/poetsorg/ poem/what-epigram.
   b. Identify two phrases Coleridge used to define an epigram.
   c. For other definitions of epigram see sites in the additional sites area cited below.
   d. Select, list, and state sources of other online definitions of epigram.
2. Find and read some e-texts of some of Donne's epigrams, or epigrammatic poems and letters.
   a. Find these e-texts at the featured websites, http://www.gutenberg. org/files/48688/48688-h/48688-h.htm and http://www.luminarium.org/ sevenlit/donne/donnebib.htm.

b. Choose one of the following works; one of Donne's epigrams such as *An Obscure Writer*, or *Disinherited*; or one of the verse letters (e.g., *Letter to the Countess of Bedford [I]*; especially the first and second lines); or one of the elegies (e.g., *His Picture*; i.e., lines 1 and 2; 3's first part; 13; 17; 19; 20).

c. Identify who Donne was writing about and something of what he said about that person.

d. How does Coleridge's epigram definition aid understanding of the chosen Donne epigram?

e. Write two new epigrammatic poems (two to six lines), being sure to work in Coleridge's defining points while considering what is said in question 3d below.

f. The first epigrammatic poem you write should be an up-to-date version of one of the subjects referred to in the works above, either the one you chose, or another one.

g. The second epigrammatic poem you write should be on an aspect of someone of historical note, or of someone who is worth remembering today, or an "average" person (of the past or present) with a worthwhile or notable memorable aspect.

3. Find and read e-texts of Ben Jonson's *Epigrams—To John Donne*; and on Donne as poet.

a. Find these e-texts at www.luminarium.org/sevenlit/jonson/benbib.htm (number XXIII) and at http://genius.com/Ben-jonson-epigram-xcvi-to-john-donne-annotated (XCVI).

b. How did Jonson characterize Donne and his writings?

c. What connection did Jonson see between their works?

d. For definitions of *wit*, including some as used in Donne's epigrams, go to https://www.litencyc.com/index.php, then search glossary for *wit* to find varied definitions through time; see also https://neoenglish.wordpress.com/2010/11/07/the-wit-of-john-donne; and more in some additional websites below.

4. Find and read an e-text of Samuel Taylor Coleridge's early nineteenth-century critical analysis poem *On Donne's Poetry*.

a. Find this e-text online at http://rpo.library.utoronto.ca/poems/donnes-poetry.

b. Identify how Coleridge precisely characterized Donne and his writings.

c. Tip: First look at lines 3 and 4, then lines 1 and 2.

5. Find some e-texts of epigram-like quotations from John Donne's works.

a. Find e-texts of these quotations at featured websites' pages including www.luminarium.org/sevenlit/donne/donnequotes.htm and in the fourth verse at www.luminarium.org/sevenlit/donne/canonization.php.

    b. Note especially the quotes beginning: "All mankind is . . .", "No Man is . . .", "Reason is . . .", "I wonder . . .", and "We'll build in sonnets. . . ."

    c. Choose three quotations, one or more of those cited in b) above, or check other web sites with quotes (e.g., https://www.goodreads.com/author/quotes/77318.John_Donne).

    d. Write essays in which you suggest what each quotation means, and why you think so.

    e. Provide examples from what you know, know about, or have heard or read about, to show your understanding.

6. Donne's writings have been identified with the literary terms *wit* and *conceit* and, in connection with these terms, he has been called a metaphysical poet, plus a "right poet."

    a. Find online definitions of, plus e-texts of noted writers and scholars' explanations of these literary terms and these types of poets and their poetry.

    b. Look online at http://www.poetryfoundation.org/learning/glossary -term/conceit, http://www.luminarium.org/sevenlit/metaintro.htm, and at additional websites below.

    c. Look for e-texts of works by noted classic writers including John Dryden, Philip Sidney, and Samuel Johnson, such as Sidney's *Defence of Poesy* (considered the first work of literary criticism) in which Donne is considered a "right poet" with his poetry a form of writing that is a *knitting up of memory*; Dryden's *Of Dramatick Poesy* in which he refers to Donne's *extravagant conceits* (also known by two other phrases); and Johnson's *Lives of the Poets* in which he refers to Donne and *conceit* and metaphysical poets (in paragraphs 3, 5, and 8 of his *Life of Cowley*).

    d. Note Dryden's reference at http://www.luminarium.org/sevenlit/ metaintro.htm; Johnson's *Lives of the Poets* at www.bartleby .com/209/775.html; plus Donne referred to in Dryden's *An Essay of Dramatick Poesy* (aka *Of Dramatic Poesie*) (1668) edited at https:// andromeda.rutgers.edu/~jlynch/Texts/drampoet.html by Jack Lynch (currently a professor at Rutgers University); and Sidney's *Apologie for Poetry* aka *Defence of Poesy* (1580, 1890) at http://www.stjohns -chs.org/english/Renaissance/Ren-si.html noting parts 3 through 9, then whole work after an 1890 introduction by A. S. Cook at https:// archive.org/details/defenseofpoesyot00sidn (especially pages 2–36, etc.). See also page 123 with comment by Dryden on Donne after book title search of *Glossary of John Dryden's Literary Terms* (1969) by H. James Jensen at http://books.google.com; and first two sentences of the 1990s item by Kaye Anfield and M. H. Abrams at www.chalacyn .com/~talyce/text/flea.html.

e. Quoting from definitions of *conceit* in e-texts of documents found online as cited above, identify features of *conceits*, including Dryden's three references.

f. Identify definitions of *wit* as stated by these commentators.

g. Identify how these classic writers defined poets; metaphysical poets, "the right poet"; "right describing note to know a poet by," and "light bringer to ignorance."

h. For more data on *conceit*, click glossary and do a word search at the https://www.litencyc.com/index.php website and see the websites http://josbd.com/conceit.html (note Samuel Johnson's, T. S. Eliot's, and Helen Gardner's comments), http://neoenglishsystem.blogspot .com (do search for Donne conceit in search box at right). Note more sites in additional websites area below.

7. As you quote from e-texts of Donne poems noted just below, and another poem by Donne that you select, explain how they are, or have, examples of *conceit* and/or *wit*, as Dryden, Johnson, Sidney, and others suggested; as noted in question/activity 6 above.

a. Look at http://allrfree.blogspot.com/2009/07/john-donne-conceit.html, then at e-texts of Donne's poems "Hymn . . . In My Sickness" (under *Divine Poems*) and "The Canonization" (under *Songs and Sonnets*) (noting verses 2 and 4 of *Canonization*) at www.luminarium.org/seven-lit/donne/donnebib.htm, then e-text of other poem here.

b. Read, identify, and explain, with quotes, comparisons involving a human body, a musical instrument, physicians, cosmographers, a patient, a map, physicians' exams, and the journey of a patient's soul.

c. Identify and explain, including quotations, the narrator's examples as he challenges someone to show that his loving someone influences or hurts things that happen in the world around him or in the world in general.

d. Identify and explain how the narrator does a turnabout and claims unusual things that people in love can cause to happen.

e. For more examples of Donne's poems being or having *conceits*: see additional sites, http://neoenglishsystem.blogspot.com/2010/11/con-ceits-and-images-of-john-donne.html.

8. Donne wrote many letters in prose and some in verse.

a. Find definitions of verse letters online at www.online-literature .com/article/donne/13732 and www.enotes.com/topics/john-donne/ critical-essays and http://www.oxfordhandbooks.com/view/10.1093/ oxfordhb/9780199218608.001.0001/oxfordhb-9780199218608-e-19.

b. See e-texts of Donne's verse letters at www.luminarium.org/sevenlit/ donne/donnebib.htm and at http://books.wwnorton.com/books/webad .aspx?id=10135, plus at additional websites with link cited below:

John Donne's Verse Letters (by first lines or persons to whom letters were written) and commentaries at http://www.oocities.org/litpageplus/donnmoul.html, and www.luminarium.org/sevenlit/donne/donnessays.htm and http://www.ipl.org/div/litcrit.

    c. Note verse letters with the first lines and "Can we find . . .", "O thou which to search, "Is not thy sacred hunger of science", "Madam", "Reason is . . .", "Sir, more than . . ., letters . . ."

    d. Identify some features of verse letters.

    e. Suggest reasons why Donne wrote verse letters.

    f. Choose a verse letter by Donne. Suggest how it is an example of why he wrote this way.

9. See in Dryden's comments the ways he said that Donne wrote on and to women.

    a. Note especially the phrase "He affects the metaphysics not only in his satires, but in his amorous verses, where nature only should reign; and perplexes the minds of the fair sex with nice speculations of philosophy, when he should engage their hearts. . . ."

    b. See an e-text of this phrase on page 6 of Dryden's *Essay on Satire* in an 1887 edition of *The Works of John Dryden,* vol.13, after book title search at http://books.google.com.

    c. Write an essay. Disagree or agree with this comment and tell why you think this way.

10. Find, read, e-text excerpts from T. S. Eliot's 1923 critical analysis on Donne and his works.

    a. See e-text after clicking link at www.luminarium.org/sevenlit/donne/donnessays.htm.

    b. Identify five comments Eliot wrote on Donne's writing then how Donne's works are relevant in modern times.

    c. Explain one comment, citing and quoting from a Donne poem e-text found online via the link at www.luminarium.org/sevenlit/donne/donnebib.htm.

11. Critic H. J. C. Grierson is also credited along with T. S. Eliot as a twentieth-century critic who revived interest and study in John Donne and his works after several centuries.

    a. Find and read online documents with comments Grierson made about Donne and his writings, as can be found at the website pages, www.bartleby.com/105/1000.html and www.bartleby.com/105/index.html, and in the Introduction and commentary to vol. 2 of *Poems of John Donne* edited by Grierson in 1912 now at https://catalog.hathitrust.org/Record/001017306 (click vol. 2 link, scroll to sections).

b. Select three comments Grierson made about Donne and Donne's writing style.

c. Find some Donne works online at featured websites, then choose one or more works that show how Grierson's comments help you gain insight into Donne's works.

12. Modern-day scholar M. Thomas Hester suggested that a phrase "a little world made cunningly" (first line of Donne's *Divine poem V* at www .bartleby.com/357/95.html) is a way to describe Donne's poems called epigrams, as indicated in Hester's article "A Little World Made Cunningly" in *The Eagle and the Dove: Reassessing John Donne* (1986), edited by Summers and Pebworth, as stated in the document at the website cited in the additional sites whose link is cited below: www.oocities .org/milleldred/donnehester2.html.

a. At http://www.luminarium.org/sevenlit/donne/donnessays.htm, click title link for The Titles/Headings of John Donne's Epigrams, and note in paragraph 4 the first part of the sentence "The title, in other words, encapsulates the subject and method of the poem in which the speaker juggles' contrasting meanings. . . ."

b. Find two items by Donne, either a brief poem, epigram, letter in verse, or quotation, as found at the featured sites, www.luminarium.org/ sevenlit/donne/donnebib.htm, www.luminarium.org/sevenlit/donne/ donnequotes.htm, www.gutenberg.org/files/48688/48688-h/48688-h .htm, and http://books.wwnorton.com/books/webad.aspx?id=10135.

c. Write an essay. How do chosen articles exemplify what Hester said of Donne's works?

13. Select another (approved) online critical analysis article from John Donne essays page at featured websites, including the *Luminarium*, *Humanities Web* pages, *Moulton's Library of Literary Criticism*, and the *Internet Public Library—Donne—Literary Criticism* section.

a. Search www.luminarium.org/sevenlit/donne/donnessays.htm, www .humanitiesweb.org (at top, click the Literature link that goes to a Library page, then click links for Sort Alphabetically, D, and Donne), http://www.ipl.org/div/litcrit, or John Donne at http://www.oocities .org/litpageplus/donnmoul.html.

b. What is the main point of the article? Refer to three points the article writer said to support a viewpoint.

c. Include quotes either from Donne's writings that the article writer stated or referred to, or that you find at featured www.luminarium.org/ sevenlit/donne/donnequotes.htm site.

Additional websites for chapter 14 with more data to note

- https://clynjohnson.wordpress.com
  - Click links to *"Discovering English Literature...* Additional Websites," then http://netedbooks.wordpress.com/home, then chapter 14, and then scroll to list.

Chapter 15

Selected Poetry by John Donne

At the *John Donne Variorum Project* website, an area of the Texas A & M University website, see authoritative e-texts of Donne's poetry in modern English; original texts in early English; transcriptions, plus explanatory notes and scholarly resources.

See works from their first publication, such as *Poems by John Donne* (1633).

See poems published during Donne's life (1572 to 1631), and others published after his death, or without dates because not known, or not published before.

More e-texts of these and other Donne poems in modern printing and spelling can be found also at other featured websites such as *Humanities Web, Luminarium, Representative Poetry Online Literature Network/Online Literature*, and *Great Books Online*.

Note phrases and words including "good-morrow," "valediction," "dreme," "riding," "anniversarie," "sonnet," and more.

For critical analyses of Donne's poems, see *Luminarium*'s essays/articles links page to items (e.g., Eliot's *John Donne*. For Jonson's writings on Donne, see Poetry Foundation web pages. See also a 2001 article by William F. Blissett in *Early Modern English Studies* and a 1999 article by Scott Nixon on Thomas Carew, Jonson, and Donne in *Web Archive's Studies of English Literature 1500–1900*.

FEATURED WEBSITES

- http://donnevariorum.tamu.edu
  - ◦ Click *Digital Facsimile Editions* link.

- ○ On next page click *1633 Edition of Poems* link or a link for the 1635 or 1669 link, then an index link, then a few title links; or click concordance link, then scroll to and click links to particular words or phrases, then click link that appears.
- ○ For other poems, see http://www.poetryfoundation.org/poems-and-poets/ poets/detail/john-donne.
- ○ Find e-text to poems by clicking link to *Donne's Poems, Articles, and More*, then *More Poems* link, then poem title link, www.humanitiesweb .org.
- ○ Click the Literature link that goes to a Library page, then click links for Sort Alphabetically, D, and Donne, John.
- ○ http://rpo.library.utoronto.ca/poets/donne-john, www.luminarium.org/sev enlit/donne (works with e-texts and audio clips), http://www.online-literature.com/donne, http://www.bartleby.com/357/22.html.
- • http://www.poetryfoundation.org/poems-and-poets/poems/detail/50676 (elegy on Donne by Jonson) and http://www.poetryfoundation.org/poems -and-poets/poems/detail/44456 ("To John Donne" by Ben Jonson).
- ○ http://www.luminarium.org/sevenlit/donne/donnessays.htm with links to, for example, http://web.archive.org/web/20030703050435/http://www. geocities.com/milleldred/donneliot.html (T. S. Eliot on John Donne), plus something on Donne and Jonson by Carew.
- ○ http://web.archive.org/web/20040518152051/http://www.geocities .com/Athens/Acropolis/6586/nixon.html, https://www.matrix.edu.au/hsc -english-module-a-john-donne-analysis.
- • http://extra.shu.ac.uk/emls/si-07/blissett.htm (note 8 and 9 on Donne and Ben Jonson).

DISCUSSION QUESTIONS AND ACTIVITIES

1. Find and read e-texts of John Donne's poems *The Good Morrow* and *A Valediction Forbidding Mourning*.
   a. Find e-texts of *The Good Morrow* and *A Valediction Forbidding Mourning* in their original printed format through index page at the http://donnevariorum.tamu.edu featured website. Find *The Good Morrow* in the 1633 edition of Donne's poems, then *Valediction* poem in the 1635 and 1669 editions. Also find e-texts in modern form on the *John Donne Pages* of the websites www.humanitiesweb.org, www.online-literature.com/donne, http://rpo.library.utoronto.ca/poets/donne-john, and www.luminarium.org/sevenlit/donne.

b. Identify, write on geographical, mathematical, astronomical references, as Donne used in relation to personal relationships between a husband and wife, as depicted in these poems.

c. Why, do you think, these references seem apt and add interesting aspects to the subject?

2. Study the first stanza of John Donne's Poem *The Good Morrow*, and stanzas four and five of *A Valediction Forbidding Mourning*.

a. Find e-texts of *The Good Morrow* and *A Valediction Forbidding Mourning* in their original printed format through index page of the 1633, http://donnevariorum.tamu.edu published edition at the featured website. Also find e-texts in modern form on the *John Donne Pages* of the websites, www.humanitiesweb.org, www.online-literature.com/donne, http://rpo.library.utoronto.ca/poets/donne-john, and www.luminarium.org/sevenlit/donne.

b. What did narrator in poem 1 think his life, a companion's life, was like before they met?

c. Identify two types of relationship between a man and woman referred to in poem 2.

3. Find and read an e-text of John Donne's poem *The Dreame*.

a. Find this e-text online in its original printed format through index page for the 1635 published edition of Donne's poems at http://donnevariorum.tamu.edu featured website.

b. Identify what Donne wrote about a dream and a particular real-life situation.

c. Imagine and write about a dream and a real-life situation you could experience. Suggest how the dream might be different from what the real-life situation would actually be.

d. Find and read e-texts of John Donne's poems including *A Valediction of His Booke* and *A Valediction of My Name, in the Window*.

e. Find these e-texts in their original printed format through an index page at the http://donnevariorum.tamu.edu featured website cited above.

f. Provide quotes. Identify in first poem what the narrator says is valuable in a book or journal.

g. Identify the astronomy metaphor and suggest its importance.

h. In the second poem, identify one of the things that a "scratch'd" or "engrav'd" name teaches.

i. Suggest what the metaphor involving "starres" means.

j. Identify what the word "valediction" means.

k. Write a poem that is your "valediction" to a subject you choose.

l. Hints: Note verse 1, line 1, then verse 4, line 2, plus verse 6, line 4, and more, of the second poem. Search at the www.infoplease.com website for a definition of the word "valediction."

4. Find and read an e-text of John Donne's poem "Good Friday 1513" [aka *Riding Westward*].

   a. At www.poetryfoundation.org/poems-and-poets/poets/detail/john-don nepoetry find an e-text of this poem by clicking link to *Donne's Poems, Articles, and More*, then *More Poems* link, then poem title link. See an e-text and end notes at http://rpo.library.utoronto.ca/poems/good-friday-1613-riding-westward and at https://tspace.library.utoronto.ca/html/1807/4350/poem654.html.

   b. Hint One: Note especially lines 1 through 12 and 33 through 34.

   c. Hint Two: Study the end notes at the *Representative Poetry Online Library* pages, http://rpo.library.utoronto.ca/poems/good-friday-1613-riding-westward and https://tspace.library.utoronto.ca/html/1807/4350/poem654.html, for general astronomical and religious data, plus Ian Lancashire's comments, especially "Is Donne serious"?

   d. Identify the astronomical references with relation to religious references, and how they relate to the narrator's life and present action.

   e. At http://crossref-it.info/textguide/metaphysical-poets-selected-poe ms/4/852, www.gradesaver.com/donne-poems/study-guide/summary -good-friday-1613-riding-westward, www.enotes.com/topics/good-fri day-1613-riding-westward, www.jstor.org/stable/2872126?seq=1# page_scan_tab_contents, and http://jamesmcgahey.blogspot.com/2012/04/john-donne-good-friday-1613-riding.html, see more commentaries on this poem.

   f. Identify various features the commentators cite in sites cited in e) just above.

   g. Write an essay on the many facets of this poem. Include its significance to you, whether with a religious viewpoint, west and east in civilization, and/or something else.

   h. At https://seanzabihi.com/2014/07/29/thoughts-on-thoreaus-walking-the-idea-of-the-west and *New Perspectives on the West* at www.pbs.org/weta/thewest/index_cont.htm, study then identify the metaphoric views on east and west. Tell how you may connect these viewpoints to parts of Donne's *Good Friday.*

5. Find and read e-texts of some of John Donne's *Holy Sonnets.*

   a. At www.poetryfoundation.org/poems-and-poets/poets/detail/john-do nnepoetry find these works' e-texts by clicking link to *Donne's Poems, Articles, and More*, then *More Poems* link, then sonnet title links or go to www.sonnets.org/donne.htm (click links).

   b. See especially lines 1 through 4 of Holy Sonnet VI, lines 1 through 6 of Holy Sonnet X, and line 1 of Holy Sonnet XIII.

c. First, quoting the phrases in the Holy Sonnets referred to just above, identify what you think Donne was writing about, and how he wrote about the subject.

d. Choose lines from one of the Holy Sonnets referred to just above, then write a poem or paragraph that features an example you think of and identify with these lines, then include a reason why you think so.

e. Tip: Your reason may be part of your poem or paragraph, or a separate statement.

f. Note: Your poem can be a rhyming couplet or four-line verse, or try challenging yourself by writing a whole sonnet.

g. Tip: For online definitions of this poetic form, visit the *Sonnet Central* website via the *Voice of the Shuttle* website at http://vos.ucsb.edu/browse.asp?id=2404 and note www.sonnets.org/17th.htm plus www.sonnets.org.

6. Find and read e-texts of John Donne's poetic tributes called the "First Anniversarie" and the "Second Anniversarie."

   a. Find these e-texts at featured sites such as http://donnevariorum.tamu.edu, www.humanitiesweb.org, and www.online-literature.com/donne http://rpo.library.utoronto.ca/poets/donne-john, and www.luminarium.org/sevenlit/donne.

   b. Write a paragraph identifying and quoting phrases he used to portray the young victim as a perfect human being and something more.

   c. Note how he related her early death to the decline of the world and the universe.

7. John Donne's writings are sometimes considered to be in two or three phases that coincide with events in his life.

   a. Study Donne bio notes on web pages such as www.humanitiesweb.org/spa/lcb/ID/42, www.luminarium.org/sevenlit/donne/donnebio.htm, www.poetryfoundation.org/poems-and-poets/poets/detail/john-donne, and www.poetseers.org/the-great-poets/british-poets/john-donne.

   b. Identify and list the two or three phases.

   c. Choose, identify, for each phase, one of Donne's poems that could belong to each phase.

   d. Write an essay, quoting from each work, and suggest why you think each one fits with his phases of life.

8. Consider John Donne's poem "Communitie," also known as "Community."

   a. Find an e-text of this poem online at featured sites including www.luminarium.org/sevenlit/donne/community.php, www.humanitiesweb.org/spa/lcp/ID/3808/c/86, www.online-literature.com/donne/358, www.bartleby.com/357/22.html, and http://rpo.library.utoronto.ca/poems/community.

b. Read and study this poem, noting especially the first two lines, then any other lines that say more on the subject as you see it. c) Write an essay. Suggest how this poem is, or parts of it are, relevant to today's world—that is, the world of the new millennium, the beginning of the twenty-first century.

9. Read some e-texts of some critical analyses of Donne and his poems.

a. Find some e-texts at http://www.luminarium.org/sevenlit/donne/don nessays.htm and at More Critical Analysis Articles on John Donne in additional websites with link below.

b. Click link on *Luminarium* web page to T. S. Eliot's essay on Donne and read the essay.

c. Go to www.poetryfoundation.org/poems-and-poets/poems/detail/44456 and http://www.poetryfoundation.org/poems-and-poets/poems/detail/50676 web pages to read Jonson's *epigrams xxiii* and *xcvi*, then read number 8 of Blissett's essay at http://extra.shu.ac.uk/emls/si-07/blissett.htm.

d. List some ways that Eliot described Donne's poetry as a group of writings.

e. Find a poem by Donne at http://donnevariorum.tamu.edu or other featured website.

f. Write an essay. Quote from a poem you chose as you aim to describe the points that Eliot as analyst wrote about Donne's poetry in general, then suggest how the poem is an example of what this analyst sees in Donne's poetry.

Additional websites for chapter 15 with more data to note

• https://www.netedbooks.wordpress.com/home
  ○ Click chapter 15, scroll to Additional Sites.

Section V

SEVENTEENTH CENTURY—PROSE

Chapter 16

"No Man Is an Island,"
"For Whom the Bell Tolls,"
and Other Writings

John Donne's prose works known as meditations, numbering twenty-three and titled *Devotions Upon Emergent Occasions* can be found online at *The Luminarium* website.

A links page features links to statement links (in numbered order) to these works.

This collection of writings by this seventeenth-century British writer, who lived from 1572 to 1631, contains a variety of musings written when Donne was ill. Featured are *Meditations upon our humane [human] condition.*

Other musings include *Prayers upon the Several Occasions* and *Expostulations and Debatements with God*, as stated in an e-text reproduction of an original printing of the book, found through a link to a digitalized publication at the featured *Luminarium* website.

An introduction to Donne's life and work, written by Izaak Walton (1593–1683), known for his biographies of churchmen and his *The Compleat Angler* (1653) (a work celebrating the countryside and the pastime of fishing), can be found online (excerpted from a full biography) at an *Anglican Library* featured web page and a review of Walton's work on Donne is at *The Inkslinger,* a blog named following a poetic statement by Byron; a statement that starts *But words are things, and a small drop of ink, falling like dew upon a thought. . . .*

To see how Donne's work translates into modern times, see web pages on twentieth-century critic T. S. Eliot's comments and twentieth-century author Ernest Hemingway's debt to Donne, plus quotes from classic the television program *The Twilight Zone*, especially an episode called The "Changing of the Guard."

FEATURED WEBSITES

- http://www.luminarium.org/sevenlit/donne/donnebib.htm
  - Scroll to *Devotions* links.
- http://www.famousliteraryworks.com/donne_for_whom_the_bell_tolls
.htm
  - See quote with well-known lines arranged as a poem from *Meditation 17.*
- Biographies at http://www.luminarium.org/sevenlit/donne/donnebio.htm and
through links at http://www.luminarium.org/sevenlit/donne/donlinks.htm
  - See Izaak Walton at http://www.ccel.org/ccel/donne/devotions.iii.html,
  http://www.anglicanlibrary.org/donne/devotions/intro.htm, https://inkslin
  gerblog.wordpress.com/2010/11/26/book-review-the-life-of-dr-john-
  donne, and https://www.poets.org/poetsorg/poet/john-donne.
- Quotations at http://www.luminarium.org/sevenlit/donne/donnequotes
.htm, http://www.luminarium.org/sevenlit/donne/alphason.htm, and http://
creativequotations.com/one/662.htm
- Donne's time: https://www.timetoast.com/timelines/107197 and http://time
rime.com/en/timeline/647915/The+Life+of+John+Donne
- For modern times and Donne, see e-texts by or about T. S. Eliot, Ernest
Hemingway, and Rod Serling's *The Twilight Zone*, at http://community
.middlebury.edu/~harris/donne.html, http://pontificating-randy.blogspot
.se/2015/01/the-twilight-zone-changing-of-guard.html.

DISCUSSION QUESTIONS AND ACTIVITIES

1. Find and read an e-text of Donne's "Meditation 17 (XVII)" from his
   Devotions Upon Emergent Occasions, noting the part with the well-known
   phrase "no man is an island" (in paragraph two).
   a. Find this e-text via featured site at www.luminarium.org/sevenlit/
      donne/meditation17.php.
   b. Identify this quotation's complete main phrase.
   c. As you refer to the metaphors Donne used, suggest what you think the
      phrase means.
2. Study further an e-text of Donne's "Meditation 17 (XVII)" from his *Devotions . . .*, noting the part with well-known phrase "for whom the bell tolls"
   (in paragraph one).
   a. Find this e-text via featured site www.luminarium.org/sevenlit/donne/
      meditation17.php.
   b. Adapt question 1 above to this quotation.
   c. Keep in mind that this quotation includes a phrase that the twentieth-
      century American writer Ernest Hemingway used as a book's title as

stated at the website, http://community.middlebury.edu/~harris/donne
.html.

    d. Suggest and compare meanings of this quotation in Donne's, and
Hemingway's works.

    e. For more data on Donne and Hemingway, see sites in additional web-
sites cited below.

3. Keep in mind the quotation from the e-text of John Donne's *Meditation 17*
from his *Devotions Upon Emergent Occasions* as referred to in question/
activity 2 above.

    a. A quote from *Meditation 17* quoted in an episode of the classic tele-
vision program *The Twilight Zone* (specifically its *Changing of the
Guard*, episode 102, last episode of season 3).

    b. Find the *Meditation* quote cited online on page 443 of *The Twilight
Zone: Rod Serling's Wondrous Land* by Kenneth Reynolds (2006),
with an analysis of the episode, after book title search at http://books
.google.com.

    c. Write an essay on what you think Donne's quote meant to this *Twilight
Zone* story.

    d. For more insight into this *Twilight Zone* episode, check website reviews
such as http://www.avclub.com/tvclub/the-twilight-zone-the-changing
-of-the-guard-99423, http://pontificating-randy.blogspot.se/2015/01/
the-twilight-zone-changing-of-guard.html, http://thescope.ca/onscreen/
the-changing-of-the-guard-the-best-of-donald-pleasence-part-2,
and http://www.twilightzonemuseum.com/show/03.php (scroll to bottom of the page).

4. Find e-texts of documents of modern literary times' people's connections to their works and Donne, such as those of T. S. Eliot and Ernest
Hemingway.

    a. Read e-texts at http://www.oocities.org/milleldred/donneliot.html,
http://community.middlebury.edu/~harris/donne.html, and http://cul
turedig.com/?p=21.

    b. Write an essay on critic T. S. Eliot's and author Ernest Hemingway's
comments on Donne. How did Donne influence them?

    c. Quote from documents by or about Eliot and Hemingway as you aim
to support your views of the influences.

5. Look at, yet again, an e-text of John Donne's *Meditation 17 (XVII)* from
his *Devotions . . .,* noting the quote that starts "all mankind is" and may
conclude with "be so translated" (in paragraph one), although clues to the
"translation" can be found in lines after noted phrases.

    a. Find this e-text via featured site at www.luminarium.org/sevenlit/
donne/meditation17.php.

    b. Suggest what the quotation means, featuring a metaphor Donne used.

    c. Write an essay with an example of a noted man or woman from modern or historic times.

    d. Suggest why you believe what Donne said is true. Refer to the quotes and the person.

6. Read an e-text of Donne's "Meditation 14 (XIV)" from *Devotions Upon Emergent Occasions.*

    a. Find e-text via featured site at www.luminarium.org/sevenlit/donne/meditation14.htm.

    b. Suggest and comment on what you think Donne referred to when he wrote about "Man's value" and "much must necessarily be presented to his remembrance."

    c. As you comment, consider that Donne was referring to humankind and more when he wrote on these subjects and connections between them: happiness, time, occasion and opportunity, cobweb, critical days, youth, a tree, the sun, birds, and seasons.

7. Read more e-text of Donne's "Meditation 4 (IV)" from *Devotions Upon Emergent Occasions.*

    a. Find e-text via featured website, www.luminarium.org/sevenlit/donne/meditation14.htm.

    b. What is a minute in a person's life (here identified as "man's life") as compared metaphorically to a minute in other features of the world?

    c. How little of life is what, and what is significant about a little of that?

    d. What of nature is metaphorically compared to something in people's lives, and how?

8. Find and choose other quotations by John Donne from his prose that you find online.

    a. Look for quotes at websites such as http://creativequotations.com/one/662.htm, http://www.luminarium.org/sevenlit/donne/donnequotes.htm, http://www.luminarium.org/sevenlit/donne/alphason.htm, and http://www.giga-usa.com/quotes/authors/john_donne_a001.htm.

    b. Suggest what Donne referred to in the quotation you chose.

    c. Explain how that quote may be apt today, as well as for Donne's time (when written).

    d. Suggest how this quotation fits with Donne's time and yet was innovative for that time.

    e. Tip: for help with understanding the world and time Donne lived in, see featured and additional bio and history sites such as www.ccel.org/ccel/donne/devotions.iii.html and http://timerime.com/en/timeline/647915/The+Life+of+John+Donne and *Unlocking the Hidden Hemingway* (2002) by Kevin Sullivan, http://fincafoundation.org/news_7.html.

Additional websites for chapter 16 with more data

- https://clynjohnson.wordpress.com
  - Click link to "*Discovering English Literature* . . . Additional Websites," then link to a wordpress.com blog at netedbooks, or go directly to http://www.netedbooks.wordpress.com/blog.

Chapter 17

Excerpts from *Juvenilia or Certaine Paradoxes and Problemes*

On this page of the *Renascence Editions Online* website, see some of John Donne's early prose works identified as his *Juvenilia* because most were written before his other writings, were distributed privately during the earlier part of his life, but published only after his death, in a 1633 first publication, and a 1652 version that his son helped to get published.

These online versions are from the Facsimile Text Society's 1936 reproduction of the first publication, in early modern English, of these *Certaine Paradoxes and Problemes* by this British writer who lived from 1572 until 1631 and worked in legal and church occupations.

Near the page's top, see a contents titles list for the *Paradoxes*, then scroll to see each part, such as *Paradox XI*, then scroll further down the page to a contents titles list for the *Problemes* and continue on for each part, such as *Probleme IV*.

Some titles and subject matter of *Certaine Paradoxes and Problemes* may seem distant from what today's students can identify with, and some parts may be disagreeable, but a few of these works, or parts of them, upon closer investigation, have something of note.

These works can be interesting, meaningful, and have something to say to people of any time. For example, an essay often paradoxically and interestingly has a view a title suggests, yet also an opposite view.

See critics' points in e-texts on *John Donne: The Critical Heritage* at Google Books with quotes. Note also e-texts of individual critics' comments, including Jonson's, Eliot's, Gardner's.

Tip: Be aware: some seemingly strange words are familiar words with early spellings.

FEATURED WEBSITES

- http://www.luminarium.org/editions/renascence/juvenilia.htm
  - Scroll to sections and also see http://catalog.hathitrust.org/ Record/001648621.
- Click full view link, then scroll to group of essays by Donne, first *Paradoxes*, then *Problemes*, all numbered.
- After a title search at http://books.google.com, see in *John Donne: The Critical Heritage* comments on what critics of the past said.
  - Click links to short comments by critics at http://spenserians.cath.vt.edu/ CommentRecord.php?action=GET&cmmtid=10493, particularly people living from 1616–1882 including Ben Jonson, John Dryden, Izaak Walton, Samuel Taylor Coleridge, and others.
  - Click links to older or modern critiques, http://www.luminarium.org/ sevenlit/donne/donnessays.htm.
  - Note critics' comments at https://quizlet.com/42705672/critics-on-john-donne-a2-english-literature-flash-cards from critics such as Samuel Johnson, T. S. Eliot, Rupert Brook, Andrew Mousley, etc.).
- http://web.archive.org/web/20010420061706/http://www.gotrice.com/ users/homework/papers/english/englit.htm see *John Donne & Tradition of English Literature* and paragraph 3; at http://web.archive.org/ web/20030703050435/http://www.geocities.com/milleldred/donneliot .html see T.S. Eliot's essay on how Donne as poet is responsible, and ways he is modern.

DISCUSSION QUESTIONS AND ACTIVITIES

1. Find and read an e-text of one of John Donne's *Paradoxes*, the one titled *Paradox XI* on the subject of the mind and body.
   a. Find this e-text online at featured website, http://www.luminarium.org/ editions/renascence/juvenilia.htm (scroll to sections).
   b. Quoting some phrases, identify why eyes and ears are important to the mind.
   c. Provide an example you can think of for each.
   d. Select worthy examples rather than those you know of just because of their popularity.
2. Find and read another e-text of one of John Donne's *Paradoxes*, such as his *Parodox X* on the subject of a laughing and a wise man.
   a. Find e-text at the featured website, www.luminarium.org/editions/rena scence/juvenilia.htm.
   b. Quoting some phrases, identify and comment on why laughing may be important to a wise man, or not.

3. Find and read an e-text of *Paradox VII* from John Donne's *Paradoxes*, found online at the http://www.luminarium.org/editions/renascence/juvenilia.htm featured website.
   a. Quoting some phrases, identify the ways Donne wrote about old men being more fantastic than young men.
   b. Tell of an example Donne wrote that seems to be a comment and the opposite viewpoint.
   c. Suggest how both viewpoints may be true.
4. Find and read an e-text of *Paradox VI* from John Donne's *Paradoxes*, found online at the http://www.luminarium.org/editions/renascence/juvenilia.htm featured website.
   a. Quote some phrases. Identify examples of when Donne actually meant "it is possible to find some vertue in women."
   b. Suggest why you think he has a positive view of women, then also an opposite view.
5. Find and read an e-text of *Paradox IV* from John Donne's *Paradoxes*, found online at the http://www.luminarium.org/editions/renascence/juvenilia.htm featured website.
   a. Quoting some phrases, identify examples of when Donne wrote "that good is more common than evil."
   b. Write a paragraph. Aim to relate something on what Donne wrote for today's world.
6. Find and read an e-text of *Paradox* VIII from John Donne's *Paradoxes*, found online at the http://www.luminarium.org/editions/renascence/juvenilia.htm featured website.
   a. Quoting some phrases, identify examples of something Donne wrote that seems to be the opposite of this *Paradox*'s title phrase "that nature is our worst guide."
   b. Tip: To help you answer a) just above, with nature viewed in two ways, note the sentences that start "Nature, though oft chased away . . . but . . ."; plus "And that poor knowledge whereby we conceive what rain is. . . ."
   c. Identify an example of something Donne wrote in this *Paradox* that fits with the *Paradox*'s title phrase.
7. Find and read an e-text of *Probleme IV: Why is There More Variety of Greene Than Other Colours* from John Donne's *Problemes*, found online at the http://www.luminarium.org/editions/renascence/juvenilia.htmfeatured website. .
   a. Quote some phrases as you identify different kinds, or shades, of green and what Donne connected them with.
   b. Suggest reasons why he made these connections.

8. Keep in mind question/activity 7 above and John Donne's *Probleme IV* of his *Problemes*, the version found online at the http://www.luminarium .org/editions/renascence/juvenilia.htm featured website.

   a. Choose another color and its different kinds or shades, or similar shades of green.

   b. Suggest your own examples that could be connected with them.

   c. Suggest and explain reasons for your choices.

9. Study some critics' comments about Donne and his writings and consider how to apply them to Donne's writings to help you understand Donne and his writing style and subjects.

   a. Find e-texts of some of these comments as the featured web-sites http://spenserians.cath.vt.edu/CommentRecord.php?action=GET &cmmtid=10493 (e.g., Ben Jonson, John Dryden, etc.); also T. S. Eliot, A. Alvarez, Helen Gardner, and more at http://www.luminarium.org/ sevenlit/donne/donnessays.htm; plus *John Donne: The Critical Heritage* after title search at http://books.google.com (with comments on, and some quotes from, these critics).

   b. Also find comments at some *Additional Websites* found via a link cited below. See H. Peters' "twinned forms" comments at http://www .jstor.org/stable/2861524?seq=1#page_scan_tab_contents, comments on "paradox as a fundamental structural device" and "an intellec-tual thrust" at http://www.phil.muni.cz/plonedata/wkaa/Offprints%20 THEPES%204/TPES%204%20(101-108)%20Kruminiene.pdf in *Pro-ceedings from Eighth Conference of British, American, and Canadian Studies*; see how Donne transformed poetry in Anca Rosu's article at http://escholarship.org/uc/item/3hg071h5, and more.

   c. See also comments on Donne's works such as "In his hands, English poetry became" at www.bartleby.com/214/1115.html, on his artful "interweaving of argument with poetry" on page 223 *Cambridge His-tory of English Literature* (1919) at http://books.google.com.

   d. Chose a *paradox* and *probleme* by Donne that you find online at the featured websites, http://www.luminarium.org/editions/renascence/ juvenilia.htm or http://catalog.hathitrust.org/Record/001648621.

   e. Write an essay. Cite and comment on some chosen Donne works' points, and critics' points at sites cited in b) above. How do they reveal something of what he wrote on?

Additional websites for chapter 17 with more data to note

- https://clynjohnson.wordpress.com
  - Click link to "*Discovering English Literature* . . . Additional Websites," then link to https://www.netedbooks.wordpress.com/home then link to chapter 17, then scroll down for list of additional websites.

EIGHTEENTH CENTURY—
MISCELLANEOUS

Chapter 18

Selections from Preface to *A Dictionary of the English Language, The Rambler, The Idler,* and *The Adventurer*

At featured websites with *Eighteenth Century E–Texts*, as on a Rutgers University English Literature page, and on a University of Australia page, see links to writings by Samuel Johnson (1709–1784), noted eighteenth-century British writer, compiler of the first important English-language dictionary, and a frequently quoted literary figure called second only to Shakespeare.

Note links to his works including *A Preface to a Dictionary of the English Language* (1755), essays from *The Rambler, Idler,* and *Adventurer* magazines, his biographical *Lives of the English Poets* including the noteworthy Alexander Pope and John Milton with critical analyses, his *Preface to Shakespeare* (1765), and his *Political Essays* including "The Patriot."

See also links to travel essays collectively titled *A Journey to the Western Islands of Scotland* (1775), and fiction, including *Rasselas, A Prince of Abissinia* (1759), plus links to his poems such as *The Vanity of Human Wishes* (1749), *Drury Lane Prologue* (1747), and *One and Twenty.*

For more poems and essays, click the *One and Twenty* poem link at Rutgers University site, scroll to search Google box, or click Google search box at Adelaide University site.

Search for poems cited in Question 5 below, and essays cited in question 3 below, and more, after clicking the www.online-literature.com website link.

Note also wit in e-texts of anecdotes and letters by Johnson; of people he knew who wrote of anecdotes he said; what commentators wrote of him; what he said of other writers and how he influenced some of them, plus why his time was called the "Age of Johnson."

FEATURED WEB SITES

- http://andromeda.rutgers.edu/~jlynch/18th/j.html#johnson Scroll to and click title links https://ebooks.adelaide.edu.au/j/johnson/samuel.
- Do Google searches via *One and Twenty* page through Rutgers site, or at Adelaide site, or scroll at http://allpoetry.com/Samuel-Johnson to *The Young Author* and *The Winter's Walk* near page's bottom or see at www.online-literature.com/samuel-johnson/johnsons-poetical-works/7, *A Word to the Wise*, or see *Lines Written Under a Print Representing Persons Skaiting* at www.online-literature.com/samuel-johnson/johnsons-poetical-works/33.
- *Guide to Quotes* at *Johnson Sound Bite Page*, www.samueljohnson.com/topics.html, http://todayinsci.com/J/Johnson_Samuel/JohnsonSamuel-Quotations.htm, letters.
- Collected by Hester Lynch Thrale Piozzi and found via http://google.com, http://literarydevices.net/anecdote, and https://web.cn.edu/kwheeler/lit_terms_A.html, http://literarydevices.net/aphorism.
- For *Age of Johnson*, see VIII (i.e., parts 4, 26–30, and more) at www.bartleby.com/220 and http://neoenglishsystem.blogspot.com/2010/12/age-of-johnson-1744-1784.html.
- For bio-sketches, see www.reocities.com/sschaeff/SamuelJohnsonintroductorypage.htm and www.archive.org/details/lifeofsamueljohnpt02bosw (with annotated chapters) by Boswell; *An Introduction to Dr. Johnson* by Frances Burney in a chapter at http://www.gutenberg.org/files/5826/5826-h/5826-h.htm#link2H_4_0008, and at https://archive.org/details/drjohnsonfannybu00bur.
  - Flip pages for *Johnsonian Passages From the Works of Fanny Burney* plus at http://books.google.com see *Early Journals and Letters of Fanny Burney,* volume 3; note *Literary Remains of Mrs. Piozzi (Thrale)* at http://www.gutenberg.org/files/15045/15045-h/15045-h.htm.
  - Note https://austensmansfield.wordpress.com/2010/09/30/literary-allusions-dr-johnsons-celebrated-judgment, "Jane Austen's Literary Relations" (illustration) at http://www.pemberley.com/janeinfo/austinfl.html.
  - C. S. Lewis on Johnson and Austen at http://www.theloiterer.org/ashton/polar_bear.html#Lewis (named after Jane's brother's publication), page 552 of *A Critical Companion to Jane Austen* by William Baker (2008) at http://books.google.com, and the document "Moral Education in Jane Austen's Novels—the Influence of Samuel Johnson" at https://www.duo.uio.no/handle/10852/25470.
  - See Leslie Stephen's *Samuel Johnson* after title search at http://books.google.com, noting *Johnson's Writings, Literary Career*; see also Macaulay on Johnson at https://archive.org/details/lordmacaulaysess-00maca with notes by Francis Storr in an 1892 edition and Macaulay on Johnson on pages 55–97 at

https://ia800300.us.archive.org/26/items/selectessaysmac02thurgoog/select-essaysmac02thurgoog.pdf with page 82 on Johnson's conversational style in 1895 Samuel Thurber edited ed. plus pages 2, 3, 46 of *Eighteenth Century British Poets and Their Twentieth Century Lives* by Thomas Simons at http://books.google.com with critics W. Jackson Bate, Lionel Trilling, in Bate's *Samuel Johnson* 1998, Trilling in *Critics in the Modern World* 2014 at amazon.com.

DISCUSSION QUESTIONS AND ACTIVITIES

1. Find and read e-text of Samuel Johnson's *Preface to a Dictionary of the English Language.*
   a. Find this e-text found online at the Rutgers University *Eighteenth Century E–Texts* featured website http://andromeda.rutgers.edu/~jlynch/18th/j.html#johnson.
   b. Identify Johnson's reasons for compiling the dictionary and some features he put in it.
   c. Include quotations from the preface as you answer b) above.
2. Select e-texts of six quotes on different topics from more than one work by Samuel Johnson such as his magazine essays, letters, lives of poets, and Boswell's biography of him.
   a. Find these quotes online at *Topical Guide to Quotes* on the *Samuel Johnson Sound Bite Page* at www.samueljohnson.com/topics.html or at http://todayinsci.com/search.htm (type Samuel Johnson in search site-wide search box, click links to Samuel Johnson science quotes), and something from *Letters to and from the Late Samuel Johnson* published in two volumes from original manuscripts in possession of Hester Lynch Thrale Piozzi (1788). Find online via contents after http://books.google.com title search (with s letter in manuscript looking like f) with subjects such as frugality, praise versus flattery, reflections on advancement of knowledge, and his opinions on his and others' travels (noting, e.g., pages 31, 64, 92, 103, 295).
   b. Write an essay where you identify each work and its subject; tell what the author aimed to say.
   c. Suggest something for each that you think is an example of, or related topic on, each subject as presented in the quotation.
3. Find definitions of the words "anecdote" and "aphorism," then e-text examples about Samuel Johnson by biographer James Boswell, then by acquaintance Mrs. Thrale by subjects.
   a. Look for definitions of anecdote and aphorism at http://literarydevices.net/anecdote and http://literarydevices.net/aphorism, then write an essay describing what they are.

    b. Find and note an anecdote about Johnson by his biographer James Boswell, found at http://www.reocities.com/sschaeff/SamuelJohn soninintroductorypage.htm, with an e-text of Boswell's brief *Characterization of Dr. Samuel Johnson.*

    c. Find anecdotes about Johnson by Mrs. Thrale Piozzi at http://books .google.com. Do title search for *Johnsoniana: Anecdotes of the Late Samuel Johnson During the Last Twenty Years of His Life* (1786 and 1882) or *Anecdotes of the Late Samuel Johnson* by Hester Lynch Thrale, later Mrs. Piozzi, and note subjects in contents of an 1884 version edited by Robinia Napier, found at http://books.google.com. See also https:// en.wikipedia.org/wiki/Anecdotes_of_the_Late_Samuel_Johnson.

    d. How did biographer James Boswell characterize Samuel Johnson with an anecdote?

    e. Choose and quote three anecdotes Mrs. Thrale used to describe Samuel Johnson.

4. Study paragraphs and phrases and select three from three different essays from Samuel Johnson's 1750s writings in the *Rambler, Idler,* and *Adventurer* magazines.

    a. Find e-texts at http://andromeda.rutgers.edu/~jlynch/18th/j .html#johnson featured site.

    b. Write an essay in which you suggest meanings in some paragraphs and phrases.

    c. Suggest some things as examples of what he said in these paragraphs and phrases.

    d. Choose, for example, "Adventurer 138," "Vulture" from *Idler,* and selected *Rambler* essays (e.g., 9, 13, 22, 36, 41) with subjects noted under "front matter."

    e. Write an essay. Quote from three Johnson essays and critics' analyses. Suggest how essays in the *Adventurer, Idler,* and *Rambler* are different. Consider style and subject.

5. Choose and read an e-text of one of Samuel Johnson's travel essays whose collection is titled *A Journey to the Western Islands of Scotland* (1775).

    a. Find e-text at http://andromeda.rutgers.edu/~jlynch/18th/j.html#johnson featured site. b) Select an e-text of, for example, "Loch Ness," "Inverness, "Glasgow," "Aberdeen," "Loch Lomond," "St. Andrews," or another travel essay in the collection.

    b. Write an essay in which you quote phrases as you identify features in a vivid word portrait of the place in the e-text essay you chose.

    c. Being guided by the ways Johnson described a place, write your own travel essay about, or a feature of, a place that you know (have lived in or visited) or have read about.

6. Find, read, and study some e-texts of some of Samuel Johnson's poems.
   a. Find these e-texts online at http://andromeda.rutgers.edu/~jlynch/18th/j
      .html#johnson featured website through links that lead to, for example,
      The Poetry Archives. Do Google searches at links via *One and Twenty*
      page at Rutgers or through Adelaide site.
   b. Read an e-text of *Vanity of Human Wishes* (1749) and two e-texts of
      his other poems (e.g., "Drury Lane Prologue," "Winter's Walk," "Lines
      Written Under a Print Representing Persons Skaiting," "One and
      Twenty," "The Young Author," "A Word to the Wise").
   c. Write an essay on "The Vanity of Human Wishes."
   d. As you write the essay, quote specifically the poem's verses' main points.
   e. Quote one point. Explain how something outside the poem is an exam-
      ple of what the poem says.
   f. For the two other poems you chose before, identify the main point of
      each poem, including quotations from them, and provide examples to
      illustrate the point.
7. Find, choose, and read a chapter from an e-text of Johnson's novel *Rasselas* (1759).
   a. Find this e-text at http://andromeda.rutgers.edu/~jlynch/18th/j
      .html#johnson or https://ebooks.adelaide.edu.au/j/johnson/samuel fea-
      tured websites.
   b. Select www.bibliomania.com website via Rutgers site to see links to
      chapters by titles.
   c. Choose a chapter title such as "The Prince Finds a Man of Learning,"
      "The Prince and Princess Leave the Valley," and "See Many Wonders,"
      "The Happiness of a Life Led According to Nature," or another chapter.
   d. Write an essay on the chapter you chose.
   e. Quoting from that chapter, identify its main point, while pointing out
      a twist.
   f. Suggest what the point's importance is in the story and to the main
      character.
   g. How may this point be important in real life?
8. In his *Preface* to *The Works of Shakespeare* (1765), Johnson wrote about
   what became basic features of literary criticism.
   a. Find and read an e-text of the "Preface" via the Rutgers or Adelaide
      featured websites.
   b. Write an essay. Identify, describe, and comment on, with examples,
      three features of literary criticism he wrote about.
   c. Tip: Write about, for example, "the three unities," "the mirrour of life,"
      "instruct by pleasing" or other ideas, as in Lynch's abridged Johnson
      "Preface" and its nos. 85, 86, and 87 found online at https://andromeda
      .rutgers.edu/~jlynch/Texts/prefabr.html.

d. Tip: Your comments should include something quoted from Shakespeare's works.

e. Hint: Note web pages with Lynch's abridged version of the *Preface* and *Johnson Timeline of Everyday Life, 1730–1800* at www.samuel-johnson.com/timeline.html.

9. Find, choose, and read e-texts of critical analysis essays or biographical comments by Samuel Johnson about other writers before or during his time.

a. Look for e-texts of essays or letters by Johnson on other writers including Alexander Pope, John Milton, Jonathan Swift, John Dryden; plus e-texts of writings by Johnson on some other writers including Frances Burney, Jane Austen, and Hester Piozzi.

b. Find e-texts of his essays through the Rutgers and Adelaide featured websites by doing a search for individual names or the collective title *Lives of the English Poets*, or via links at https://en.wikipedia.org/wiki/Lives_of_the_Most_Eminent_English_Poets.

c. See also writings about Johnson and Burney in Freya Johnston's *Making an Entrance: Fanny Burney and Samuel Johnson* including page 189 in *A Celebration of Fanny Burney* (2007) ed. by Lorna J. Clark after book title search at http://books.google.com, on pages xxv and 497 in *Samuel Johnson: A Biography* (2008) by Peter Martin, *Dr. Johnson and Fanny Burney* (1911) by Chauncey Brewster Tinker at https://archive.org/details/drjohnsonfannybu00bur, and *The Condition of Women* (especially page 83) in *Cambridge Companion to Samuel Johnson* (1997) by Greg Clingham after title search for *Companion* at http://books.google.com, plus *Letters by Samuel Johnson* (e.g., vol. III page 14 note 4 and page 196, plus vol. V Index with list of letters with dates after search for Frances Burney) at http://books.google.com then search in *Letters of Samuel Johnson* (1892) ed. by George Birkbeck Hill at https://archive.org/stream/lettersjohnson01hilluoft#page/n5/mode/2up; plus writings on Johnson and Austen through links at http://www.theloiterer.org/ashton/ardatJ.html.

d. Find and read e-texts of works by two writers and how they had connections with Johnson.

e. For connections, note Gloria Gross's "Mentoring Jane Austen: Reflections on 'My Dear Dr. Johnson's'" at www.jasna.org/persuasions/printed/number11/gross.htm and https://doughertyeng275.wordpress.com/2011/10/16/jane-austen-and-samuel-johnson; Burney and Johnson in *A Celebration of Fanny Burney* at http://books.google.com, pages ix–xi, 437 in *Early Journals and Letters of Fanny Burney,* volume 3 (1779) at http://books.google.com; plus something on style in the *Lives of the English Poets* essays at https://andromeda.rutgers.

edu/~jlynch/Johnson/Guide/lives.html and names of the most important lives as noted at the wikipedia.org page cited in b) just above.

f. Write an essay. Comment on how Johnson's critical analysis essays
or comments, and scholars' or noted biographers' comments, help you
understand what Johnson aimed to say about these writers.

10. Find e-text excerpts from biographical writings on Johnson by James
Boswell, Frances (Fanny) Burney D'Arblay, Jane Austen, Thomas B.
Macauley, and Leslie Stephen.

a. See Boswell's comments at www.reocities.com/sschaeff/Samuel-
Johnsonintroductorypage.htm, www.archive.org/details/lifeofsamu-
eljohnpt02bosw (with annotated chapters), and www.gutenberg.org/
files/1564/1564.txt (abridged version).

b. See Macauley's comments on pages 55–97, noting conversational
style on page 82, at https://ia902308.us.archive.org/23/items/lord-
macaulaysess00maca/lordmacaulaysess00maca.pdf, with notes by
Francis Storr; and note pages 16-52 at https://archive.org/details/
lordmacaulaysess00maca; both being versions of Macauley's *Essay
on Boswell's Biography of Johnson.*

c. See Stephen's comments at https://zhiv.wordpress.
com/2009/09/27/91809-samuel-johnson-leslie-stephen-and-virginia-
woolf, noting last two sentences of paragraph two and following paragraphs; noting chapters 2 and 4 at http://www.readcentral.com/book/
Leslie-Stephen/Read-Samuel-Johnson-Online and at www.cambridge.
org/zw/academic/subjects/literature/english-literature-1700-1830/
samuel-johnson see a description of a book on *Samuel Johnson* (1878)
written by Leslie Stephen, father of author Virginia Woolf; plus see
Leslie Stephen 1878 biography of Johnson at the archive.org essays
featured website, noting Stephen on *Johnson's Writings, Literary
Career, As Literary Dictator.*

d. See Burney's comments at http://www.gutenberg.org/
files/5826/5826-h/5826-h.htm#link2H_4_0008 with *An Introduction
to Dr. Johnson,* and how Burney was inspired by Johnson, what
she thought of him; plus at https://archive.org/details/drjohnson-
fannybu00bur see *Johnsonian Passages From the Works of Fanny
Burney,* and see *Early Journals and Letters of Fanny Burney,* vol.
3 at http://books.google.com, http://essays.quotidiana.org/burney/
learned_man_on_evelina.

e. See some Austen comments and references on Johnson at https://
austensmansfield.wordpress.com/2010/09/30/literary-allusions-dr-
johnsons-celebrated-judgment, "Jane Austen's Literary Relations"
(illustration) at http://www.pemberley.com/janeinfo/austinfl.html,
C. S. Lewis on Johnson and Austen at http://www.theloiterer.org/

ashton/polar_bear.html#Lewis, and page 552 of *A Critical Companion to Jane Austen* by William Baker (2008) at http://books.google. com; https://austensmansfield.wordpress.com/2010/09/30/literary-allusions-dr-johnsons-celebrated-judgment, "Jane Austen's Literary Relations" (illustration) at http://www.pemberley.com/janeinfo/ austinfl.html, C. S. Lewis on Johnson and Austen at http://www. theloiterer.org/ashton/polar_bear.html#Lewis, see at http://books. google.com "Critical Companion to Jane Austen" (2008) by William Baker, with a search inside for *Johnson, Samuel* and then going to page 552, then at www.amazon.com doing search for audio clip of Austen's poem "To the Memory of Mrs. Lefroy" with third verse on Johnson, plus others' comments on Austen and Johnson at http://www.jasna.org/persuasions/printed/number11/gross.htm, http:// www.journals.uchicago.edu/doi/abs/10.1086/391209?journalCode =mp, and https://www.questia.com/library/journal/1G1-178617008/ who-evaluates-whom-and-what-in-jane-austen-s-novels

   f. Write an essay. Including quotes, identify some things that Boswell, Burney, Austen and Piozzi, Stephen, Macauley, Bate, and Trilling wrote on Johnson and/or his works in *Critics in the Modern World*.

11. A literary age was named for Samuel Johnson at the time he lived, wrote, and shortly after.

   a. Find and read the first two paragraphs of the e-text at the featured websites www.bartleby.com/220 (VIII, 4, 26–30), and http://neoeng lishsystem.blogspot.com/2010/12/age-of-johnson-1744-1784.html.

   b. Helped by section VIII parts at featured bartleby.com web pages cited above and the last sentence in paragraph two at the neoenglishsystem site, identify *Age of Johnson* traits.

   c. Write an essay, with quotations, about how you think Johnson's poems *London* and *A Vanity of Human Wishes*, found through the Rutgers featured site, exemplify this *Age*.

Additional websites for chapter 18 with more data to note

- https://clynjohnson.wordpress.com
  - Click link to *Discovering English Literature* . . . Additional Websites, then link to http://netedbooks.wordpress.com/home.

Conclusion

This book, "British Literature—The Beginnings" (volume 1 of a three-part series: "Discovering English Literature in Bits and Bytes: An Internet Approach") provides a unique way for secondary school students and beginning college and university students to discover in today's times, literature in English from the beginning, and then throughout history, as well as into the new millennium (as hinted at in questions and activities by this book's author).

A unique array of literary forms has dotted the landscape during the beginnings of English literature, from about 600 AD to the end of the eighteenth century—as this volume (series 1, volume 1) demonstrates. Early documents reveal a great variety. There are runes and charms, like intriguing puzzles which educate and entertain. Travel writings, including essays, stories, and poems, allow readers to experience journeys, as with "The Seafarer's Journey," the epic *Canterbury Tales* by Geoffrey Chaucer, starting with when April comes "and many little birds make melody . . . folk do long to go on Pilgrimage"; plus Samuel Johnson's "Journey to the Hebrides" [in Scotland] and "Loch Ness"; plus Shakespeare's "undiscovered country."

There are ancient letters that investigate the nature of knowledge and learning between secular and religious leaders; and "talking poems" by one of England's first kings, showing his human side as he grows up, while mirroring something of his nation.

There are early folk or fairy tales emerging as metaphors and allegories as in Edmund Spenser's *Faerie Queene*.

Letters in verse such as those to a Countess of Bedford, and meditations on "emergent occasions," highlight John Donne's works, as shown at the *Bartleby: Great Books Online, Project Gutenberg: Plain Text Archive,*

Luminarium: Anthology of English Literature, and other websites and digital databases.

Poems within plays or dramatic poetry as well as iconic dramatizations and model sonnets showcase William Shakespeare, along with another kind of unique sonnet by Spencer.

Then there is the "Age of Johnson" with Dr. Samuel Johnson's anecdotes and dictionary and the iconic biography of him by James Boswell.

And then there is the entrance of Jane Austen onto the literary scene . . . with her early letters to her sister and to an acquaintance (Mrs. Hester Lynch Thrale Piozzi) who held literary gatherings that had featured Dr. Johnson, then Jane starting her novels. Beginnings of references to Johnson, his works, and his style appear in her writings and literary viewpoints, although he had died before she became a teenager.

From Great Britain and the United States, extending to Canada and some Pacific Ocean islands, this book, and its companions, offer a modern day way that aims to present original literary documents, and their messages, written by iconic literary lights through time, written for their times and beyond, and provided and reproduced for today's world on the Internet in digitized formats whether in original writings or printed/transliterated reproductions.

Chapters present urls of suggested databases to visit, then offer questions and activities that spark critical thinking on, and accompany references to, quotations from the documents—all from the perspective of the books' author/scholar, with viewpoints shaped primarily by British and American literary icons such as Madeleine L'Engle, T. S. Eliot, Emily Dickinson, J. R. R. Tolkien, Robert Frost, Rachel Carson, and others, with some quotes from their writings.

In ways reflecting metaphorically and literally how a contemporary invention—the Internet—can introduce historical literary documents to today's students, the chapters in this book (as do all chapters in all volumes of the series) reveal the significance of whole historical documents (some of the writers' body of work) and quotations from them through time, plus, moreover, in today's society.

For examples, look for origins of ancient British riddles and how they are woven in unique new ways into modern and contemporary British writings by J. R. R Tolkien and J. K. Rowling; find out how Shakespeare's original plays have been interwoven into modern and contemporary popular literary creations—as with television's iconic *Star Trek* episodes and see how literary works from literary history have significance in modern times' television's noteworthy series such as the *Twilight Zone*, as well as *Gilmore Girls*, and *Lost*.

Note also historical literary figures known today through movies and spin-offs of their works, while noting how these figures first made their marks—as with Jane Austen and the literary circle she early became part of, which included her literary mentor Samuel Johnson with his dictionary, adventurer and rambler essays, plus "The Story of Rasselas, Prince of Abissinia" at the *Online Books Page* website with links to the *Hathi-Trust Digital Library*, "*Journey to the Hebrides*" at the *Internet Digital Archive*, plus Frances Birney d'Arblay's letters and diaries with tidbits on Johnson as provided by the *Electronic Text Center* at the *University of Virginia/Wayback Machine* site, and Hester Lynch Piozzi who wrote of "The Anecdotes of the Late Samuel Johnson" as provided at the *Project Gutenberg* website.

The key to bringing early writings and recent writings into the present can be seen well through the Internet and the guidance provided by the "Discovering English Literature in Bits and Bytes" series of books, as has been initially indicated in the paragraphs above, and in this book, volume 1: *English Literature: British Literature—Beginnings*, that is using online features including databases such as "*Luminarium: Anthology of English Literature*," "*Northvegr*" (the "*Northern Way*") with "*Miscellaneous Primary Sources—Anglo-Saxon Charms*" plus "*Forgotten Ground Regained: A Treasury of Alliterative and Accentual Poetry*"; "*Chaucer: Manuscripts and Books on the Web*," "*Resources for the Study of Edmund Spenser*," "*Shakespeare On the Net*," "*The Works of John Donne*," "*Samuel Johnson Sound Bite Page*," plus the *Jane Austen Society of North America* database, and the *Jane Austen Pemberly* database, with Austen, although born just nine years before his death, being considered "Johnson's most distinguished student" (in Boswell's *The Life of Johnson*, v. 2, page 141); Gloria Gross's 1989 "Mentoring Jane Austen: Reflections on 'My Dear Dr. Johnson's web document; an abstract of a 2006 thesis: "*Moral Education in Jane Austen's Fiction: the Influence of Dr. Johnson*" by Lena Blakkisrud, plus a page on the twentieth century's literary icon C. S. Lewis's comment halfway down the page of a connection between Johnson and Austen in *The Voices of Men On Jane Austen* website, along with her letters including phrases such as "like my dear Dr. Johnson, I believe I have dealt more with Notions than Facts" (from a February 8 letter to her sister), plus in her poem ("To the Memory of Mrs. Lefroy") with lines that claim no one is second to, or can be a substitute for, him; also, as a brother and nephew claimed, Jane's "favourite author in prose" was Dr. Johnson, as quoted in "*Mentoring Jane Austen*."

Other hints of his influence in her writings and other people's (e.g., C. S. Lewis, Cornel West), suggest influences such as Austen being Johnson's and Shakespeare's "literary daughter" or Johnson's "literary critical daughter"; with her references to Johnson's dictionary and essays woven into her fiction in ways "not so much quoted but echoed and reflected, and that not infrequently" as stated by a James Battersby as quoted in "*The Friendly Jane Austen*" by Natalie Tyler in Google Books.

Also, Austen's way of writing seems to have been anticipated in a *Rambler* essay by Johnson, written before she was born. In it he stated: "The works of fiction with which the present generation seems more particularly delighted, are such as exhibit life in its true state, diversified only by accidents that daily happen in the world, and influenced by passions and qualities which are to be found in conversing with mankind. . . . Its province is to bring about natural events by easy means, and to bring up curiosity without the help of wonder: it is therefore precluded from the machines and expedients of the heroic romance. . . ." [at www.theloiterer.org/ashton/year00/post500a.html, a site with a title of her brothers' publication].

Meanwhile hints of the importance of Austen in the twenty-first century, further explored in series 1, volume 2 of the "Discovering English Literature in Bits and Bytes" books, is suggested by modern scholar, fervent political debater, and sometimes Bernie Sanders supporter, Cornel West, who comments that Austen had "the power to look within, and to change, to transform society from the inside" [as stated at www.huffingtonpost.com/kathleen-anderson/why-cornel-west-loves-jan_b_6140744.html].

Perhaps explainable more succinctly or precisely, it may be said in the words of recent writers who delve/have delved into the past as they write/or wrote of and during the recent past or present. Consider some modern writers who have brought the ancients into the present uniquely, while looking and venturing forward. Think of, for example, the iconic writer Madeleine L'Engle's comment: "life is like a sonnet . . ."; Jane Austen's forward-looking character Mr. Darcy saying "To all this [attainments Miss Bingley thought necessary for accomplished women], she must yet add something more substantial, in the improvement of her mind by extensive reading."

There are also Donne's "No man is an island entire of itself" in Rod Serling's science fiction classic television program: *Twilight Zone*: "The Changing of the Guard" set in a boys' school, and the start of comments by Austen on Johnson, plus beginnings of studies of Johnson's writings influencing Austen.

Then there is Tolkien's riddle poem "The road goes ever on and on . . . / and whither then? I cannot say"; while Shakespeare's Hamlet says "There are more things in heaven and earth . . . than are dreamt of in your [or, some say, our] philosophy."

Appendix 1

More Websites to Note

https://netedbooks.wordpress.com/

BY TOPIC

https://lynlibrarianwriter.wordpress.com/2013/11/15/introducing
-critical-thinking-through-american-literature-on-the-net/

ADJUNCT LIST OF WEBSITES

https://discoverenglitonline.wordpress.com/2016/08/06/adjunct-list-of-web
-sites-to-go-with-introduction-to-all-volumes-of-the-12-book-series-discov
ering-english-literature-in-bits-bytes-an-internet-approach-to-british-and
-american-literature/

Index

and *Threading Shakespeare's
Sonnets* (Bennett), 89, 90
See also Sonnets, Shakespearean,
89–95
his sonnets by first lines, 93
his sonnets by number (e.g., 12, 14,
15, 17, 21, 33–35, 38, 64, 65), 93
his sonnets by title
How heavy do I . . . (50 or L), 92
Let us not to . . . (116 or CXVI),
92
Like as the waves . . . (60 or LX),
92
Love is too . . . (151 or CLI), 92
Not Marble, nor . . . (55 or LV),
91, 92
Shall I compare thee . . . (18 or
XVIII), 92
Some Glory in . . . (91 or XCI),
91
*Sonnets to Sundry Notes of
Music*, 83, 85
That Time of Year . . . (73 or
LXXIII), 92
When in disgrace . . . (29 or
XXIX), 92
When to the sessions of . . . (30
or XXX), 92
his subjects in his sonnets, 93, 94
his themes in his sonnets, 93
his tragic plays, 73–80
Antony and Cleopatra, 73, 75,
76, 77
Hamlet, 73, 74, 75, 76, 77, 78
Julius Caesar, 73, 75, 76, 78
King Lear, 73, 75
Macbeth, 73, 74, 75, 76
Othello, 77
Romeo and Juliet, 73, 75, 76, 77
miscellaneous
and *De Shakespeare A T.S. Eliot*
(Fluchere), 62
and Francis Bacon, 64
and *Literary Remains of
Shakespeare* (Coleridge), 90
and literary vocabulary, 86

and quotations, 69, 70, 71, 87
and *The British Library*, 89
and *Hollywood Bard*, 63
and *Men vs. Women: Examining
Relationship between Genre
and Gender in Shakespeare?*
(Kurzawski), 61
and *The Oxford Shakespeare*, 83
and PBS and Shakespeare, 83
and *Portrayals of Children in
Shakespeare's Plays*, 67
and *Preface to Shakespeare*
(Johnson), 58, 62
and *Rise of Poetic Interpretation
in Shakespeare*, 83, 84
and *A Sentence from Shakespeare*
(Huxley), 71
and *Search for Transcendence in
Shakespeare* (Eliot), 69
and *Shake Sphere: A
Comprehensive Shakespeare
Study Guide*, 57
and *Shakespeare and the
Classical Tradition*, 58
and *Shakespeare, His Mind and
Art* (Dowden), 62
and *Shakespeare's Life, Times,
and Places*, 73
and *Shakespeare Navigators*, 65,
66, 70
and *Shakespeare on the Internet*,
58
and Shakespeare's Dramatic Art
Form
and *Shakespeare's Influence On
Other Artists*, 66, 71
and *Shakespeare's Last Plays*
(Freeh), 69
and *Shakespeare's Use of
Language*, 84, 86
and *Shakespearean Code or
Cipher*, 64, 66
and *Shakespearean Code*
references, 64, 66, 72
and *Shakespearean Monologues*,
65

About the Author

Carolyn M. Johnson is author of reference and textbooks including *Using Internet Sources to Teach Critical Thinking Skills in the Sciences* for secondary and beginning college and university students and "Discovering Nature with Young People"; plus magazine articles, poems, puzzles, and reviews *SJU Graduate English Newsletter, Modern Haiku, Library Journal, New Library Scene, Christian Library Journal,* and *Abstracts of English Studies.* She has MLS (Library and Information Science) and MA (English and American Literature) degrees from St. John's University, Queens, NY, a BA (English Literature) from Hunter College, NYC, and an AA (Liberal Arts) from Queensborough Community College, Queens, NY; she has worked as a graduate student assistant in the LIS Division at St. John's University, library assistant at QCC library, and librarian at NY Botanical Garden Library and Pace University Library.

www.ingramcontent.com/pod-product-compliance
Lightning Source LLC
LaVergne TN
LVHW042335060326
832902LV00006B/180